BORN UNBREAKABLE

Born Unbreakable

5 STEPS TO OVERCOMING YOUR SELF-LIMITING BELIEFS

DESIREE MAYA

Post Hill
PRESS

A POST HILL PRESS BOOK
ISBN: 979-8-88845-404-6
ISBN (eBook): 979-8-88845-405-3

Born Unbreakable:
5 Steps to Overcoming Your Self-Limiting Beliefs
© 2024 by Desiree Maya
All Rights Reserved

Cover design by Conroy Accord

This is a work of nonfiction. All people, locations, events, and situations are portrayed to the best of the author's memory.

Post Hill Press
New York • Nashville
posthillpress.com

Published in the United States of America
1 2 3 4 5 6 7 8 9 10

This book is dedicated to my nieces Jacqui and Jasmine who remind me that the future is bright.

And...

To my late father for showing me the meaning of discipline.

To my mother for teaching me the value of compassion.

To my sister for instilling in me the strength of perseverance.

This book is written for those who feel like they are not enough. It's for the people who have questioned their worthiness. It's for the people who have the desire to overcome their limitations.

Don't fret. You can and will grow in ways that you never thought imaginable.

CONTENTS

FOREWORD

WANT TO HAVE A LIMITLESS life? You came to the right place, and you have the right book in your hands. I have been a Business Adviser for years. I have advised, worked with, and spoken to some of the most influential people alive. It has been an honor. If I'm spilling the truth tea, at times it has been a little discouraging.

There are many out there who aren't walking the walk. They know the punch lines, they know the photos to take and with whom, but when it comes down to *do*—they don't feel like "real" people creating *real* change, which is why I am so excited to write Desiree's foreword.

I can still remember the day I met Dez Maya. It was in Columbus, Ohio, and we were at a Lewis Howes event. She had a presence to her that was undeniable. I noticed it immediately. She was a woman on a mission, but it was also clear that she intended to take others with her on this mission. Oh, and she's a fabulous dancer too. Let that be well documented.

Soon I became her advisor and coach. She was in my 5:30 a.m. mastermind for years. Let me say that again: 5:30 a.m., which was particularly brutal because she was traveling a lot for work. She'd sometimes fly in at 2:00 a.m. and still drag herself to the Zoom call with me. I was impressed, but not just by her commitment. What really struck me was how she still elevated everyone who was on that mastermind call. She poured into them, reminded them of their strengths, their successes, and the humanness of their challenges. She was so committed to being better and helping those around her be better. She'd remind Christopher of his ability to lead, Bethany of the way she dared greatly in the arena, and so many others, because at her core, she is a coach and a leader.

Just as she cared for and elevated everyone on that mastermind call, I know she cares for and will elevate you, Dear Reader. She wants you to get ahead. She has put the blood, sweat, and tears into this book so that you can stand on her shoulders. She wants to shorten your path to success and, by God, make the path a heck of a lot more fun in the process. It is an honor to witness someone like Dez get ahead because she's the exact kind of person who should. She fought hard for the lessons she teaches in this book; she earned the right to teach them.

She herself had to crush self-limiting beliefs. I watched them with my very eyes every Wednesday morning. She isn't someone who stands at the podium and lectures what she has not tested herself. This is a woman who has walked through fire and miraculously came out the other side with a smile and a leather jacket on. She is not a woman who just read a book on leadership. She is leadership. She is not a woman who read a book on grit. She is grit.

The joy in being behind the scenes with her all these years is that she is who she appears to be. When you meet many authors off stage or outside of their book signing, they are not who they appear to be, but for Dez, the opposite is true. She's even better: more loving, more inspiring, from retiring her mother to inspiring other women who may have not seen someone who looked like them on stage yet. She is the mentor we've been waiting for.

This is a book that will change you. I encourage you to grab a cup of tea and lean in. You will like the version of you that emerges on the other side.

April Garcia
Founder of PivotMe

INTRODUCTION

YOUR LIFE IS ABOUT TO change. You picked up this book, so I know you have the desire for growth. There is no better time than now.

The self-help market can feel a bit dismaying because you are trying to decipher between the people who are gimmicks and the people you can learn from based on real experiences and the genuine desire to help others. It's my burning desire to help you. I have been where you are, and I am still learning—just like you. I don't profess to be an omnipotent guru who has reached some kind of revered status in an ivory tower or the top of the highest mountain. I'm human, and I make mistakes all the time. I choose to keep getting up each time I fall, and the bottom line is that I have learned a few powerful things. I want to share those learnings with you.

We all have had or currently have beliefs that are limiting. It is easy to fall into the trap of letting those self-limiting beliefs hold us hostage, keeping us from doing what we want in life, robbing us of our peace, and making us play small when we should be playing big. Quite frankly, to stay in a limited frame of mind is exhausting. Second-guessing who we are, trying to live up to the expectations of others, punishing ourselves for our past, and striving for impossible perfection is all too heavy to bear. Do you want to carry a weight like this for the rest of your life? I don't, at least not anymore.

The principles in this book are ones I personally have tested. I am still a student of them today. They come from my personal and professional experiences—and from people I admire, many of whom I've seen personally apply them. I am a huge believer in mindset. Every action we take starts with the mind. I want you to take the position of student as you read this book and open your mind to new ways of thinking. If you do that simple task, I guarantee you'll learn a thing or two that will enable transformation in your life.

I've struggled through two divorces, I've jumped in and out of multiple multi-level marketing journeys, I've repeatedly interrogated my ability to be an entrepreneur, I've experienced the loss of a parent, I've felt less than for not fitting the societal norm of being a mother, I've questioned my identity, I've punished myself for past mistakes, and I've contemplated suicide more than once in my life. I've been in the dark depth of despair that I hope others never have to go through.

The upside to the tribulations I've shared is that I also have a fervent commitment to self-development: I'm an avid reader, faithful podcast listener, consumer of self-help videos from Technology, Entertainment, Design (TED) Talks to YouTube and everything in between, and consistent attendee to events that push me to become better. The death of my father at nine years old put me on a growth trajectory I only understood in my adulthood and am now grateful for. Life in and out of the formal classroom has positioned me as a life-long student. Nearly two decades ago, I chose a career in coaching and consulting that allows me to practice what I preach daily. Becoming a podcaster has opened the door to a plethora of learnings that are beyond my wildest dreams. This is all to say that while I have experienced tremendous pain, I know firsthand what it looks like to experience tremendous progress.

What I know for certain is that where there is darkness, there too can be light. It has taken professionals like therapists, mentors, and coaches along with wise loved ones to help me realize this. I want to call out now that if you're planning on this self-development adventure to be a solo one, stop now. You can't do this without the guidance and support of others. I'll share more about what this looks like, so keep reading. I don't profess that my personal examples will be ones that will hit close to home for you. I certainly hope that they do. As an insurance policy though, I wanted this book to be one where you can find someone to relate to; therefore, you will not only read about my personal experiences but that of others. Many of the stories come from people I've interviewed on my podcast show. My promise to you as the author of this book is that you will get at least get three things in the pages to follow: relatability, inspiration, and tactics. I will give you all of me, and now I invite you to give to yourself. You deserve what lies ahead.

1

THOSE DARN SELF-LIMITING BELIEFS

SELF-LIMITING BELIEFS. UGH. THEY CREEP into our lives, hop into the driver's seat, and sometimes accelerate at full speed. The formal definition of a self-limiting belief is "preventing the development or expression of the self." I have spent the past thirty-three months (and counting) studying self-limiting beliefs by interviewing entrepreneurs, leaders, and influencers from all over the world on my podcast, the *Born Unbreakable Podcast Show* (I will get into more details about why and how I started my brand and podcast show a little later in the book). A quick mention about podcasts in case you are unfamiliar—a podcast is an audio program (usually pre-recorded) like talk radio made available in a digital format via internet download through platforms such as Apple, Spotify, Audible, and Amazon Music to name a few. On my show, I've conducted interviews on a variety of topics that my guests are experts on (e.g., love, relationships, health, wealth, business, and so on) and led solo episodes, and most recently, I conduct co-hosted episodes. Therefore, episodes don't need to be listened to or watched sequentially, unlike a TV series where episodes are usually watched in chronological order. My podcast guests range from the ages of thirteen to seventy-plus and come from all over the world. As of the time this book is being written, 57 percent are female, and 43 percent are male. Guess what? One hundred percent of them experienced having self-limiting beliefs. I would argue that we all do.

Here are common self-limiting beliefs that might resonate with you, including examples shared by my guests:

I am not smart enough.

I am not attractive enough.

I am not good enough.

I am not capable enough.

I am not worthy.

I am not relevant.

I am not desirable.

I am not lovable.

I am an imposter.

I am limited.

I am a failure.

Do any of these statements sound familiar? All these limiting thoughts have cycled through my mind at one point or another. One limiting belief that has rung true for me throughout my life is, *I am not worthy*. I grew up in Fremont, California, nestled south of San Francisco and north of San Jose. It is a large city with a population of nearly a quarter million people. I was the younger sibling. I have a sister who is nine years older than me. I was raised in a Catholic family in both the Filipino and Hawaiian cultures. My father was an immigrant from the Philippines. As a late teenager he arrived in Hawaii, where he met my mother. He served in the U.S. Army, as did most of the men in my family. He was the breadwinner of the family, working as an insurance broker for Allstate. My mother worked in Information Technology until the dot.com crash, and then she explored other industries and ultimately planted her feet in healthcare.

The principles my father instilled in me before he passed away from a stroke when I was nine years old were the importance of academics, working hard, having faith, living in gratitude, and being obedient. I had a wonderful upbringing in a loving household, but unworthiness crept into my life when I saw my mom struggle financially as a widow managing the household on one income. She never remarried. She devoted her life to working and being a mom. I saw my sister graduate high school at age sixteen, go to college, become a flight attendant, and move out at age eighteen. I thought, "Well, this must be as good as it gets." I observed that the right thing to do was to play it safe; do not take risks, just put your head down, go to school, and land a well-paying job to become an independent, responsible adult. This path seemed reasonable, logical, and sensible. It was also the popular and socially acceptable path (the societal norm). While I knew there were other ways to live life, I wasn't intimately exposed to those different pathways.

CHOOSING SAFETY

I did all the safe things. I graduated at the top of my class at Irvington High School then went to the University of California, San Diego (UCSD) where I majored in political science and minored in healthcare and social issues. After graduating with a bachelor's degree, I became a Healthcare Consultant at a reputable consulting firm. I traveled (and still do) all over the United States solving complex performance improvement challenges. While I accomplished a fair amount, unworthiness played a role throughout every chapter of my life. I found a passion for leadership at an early age. My first leadership post was as the representative for my third-grade class at Alvarado Elementary School. By the time I graduated high school, I ran for vice president. I did not run for president because I did not think I was worthy of a job that carried the ultimate leadership responsibility; second in command could be just as fulfilling. I did the same thing in college. Senator would be a respectable yet safer role. Once again, the presidential role would be too big and too much responsibility. Behind the scenes seemed to be a good fit for me. I adopted that mindset into my consulting career: "other" leadership roles would be well-respected yet safer than being the top leadership role of managing director, who had a heavy emphasis on sales. Sales would be too overwhelming and too much pressure—no, thanks!

I realize today that being too risk-averse and playing it safe won't get me everything I want in life, but I needed to expand my experience and my circle before I believed I deserved more than what I had accepted for so long. It's easy to become a product of our environment. That is not necessarily a bad thing, but it can be a limiting thing. When I was growing up, this meant making predictable and stable choices like a college education and a career with benefits where you can have upward mobility, but don't have to run the business or company to make a lucrative living.

I recently watched a talk that Chinese American actor, stand-up comedian, and writer Jimmy O. Yang did at Google. He's well-known for his role as Bernard Tai in the movie, *Crazy Rich Asians*, and Jian-Yang in the HBO comedy series, *Silicon Valley*. Jimmy is an immigrant who was born in Hong Kong and settled in Los Angeles with his parents at age thirteen. His father invested in his future, and he just so happens to have the same alma mater as me, UCSD. He graduated with a degree in economics. Jimmy's father had expectations of Jimmy putting his degree to immediate use, and go figure, guess what kind of work he started doing after graduating? Consulting, just like me. He interned at the financial consulting firm, Smith Barney, in Beverly Hills. He was not fulfilled by the work and his heart led him down a totally different path. Jimmy had a love for comedy and pursued that passion with discipline and voraciousness. While his father was a skeptic of his decision to veer off the well-traveled path called societal acceptance, Jimmy didn't waver from his calling. Today, his career is booming in the entertainment industry. His story inspired me. Like me, he grew up in a traditional Asian culture, had a loving family, and went to a reputable university. Unlike me, Jimmy wasn't afraid to take a risk. He is an example of entrepreneurship and what can happen when you bet on yourself.

Entrepreneurship was introduced to me while I was in college through multi-level marketing companies like Pre-

Paid Legal (legal support services) and Herbalife (health and wellness supplements). I started dabbling in the notion of a side hustle and figured out that there are no limitations to what you can do if you apply your energy and effort to something. I didn't see direct examples when I was young of women who started their own businesses or ventured outside the societal norm of men being the household breadwinners. Women in my universe prioritized running a household and having a steady job that would contribute to expenses. Women were in supportive roles financially versus equal or primary roles. It wasn't until my thirties that I truly got more intimate, firsthand exposure to women-led and women-owned businesses.

Today, I see tons of examples of female entrepreneurs who inspire me, and I am much more empowered to grow my own businesses part-time (I manage a private coaching practice and co-own a production company) while maintaining a full-time corporate career. I'm on an executive committee for an organization founded by my dear friend Tammi Relyea called WO3: the WO stands for women-owned, and the 3 represents the principles of partner, promote, and support. (Do check it out: https://www.wo3connect.com.) On the last Saturday of March (Women's History Month), we celebrate women-owned businesses by spotlighting female entrepreneurs on social media throughout the month to raise awareness about their brands and foster a community of powerhouse women.

We also find ways to partner, promote, and support women-owned businesses; this could be through publicizing or purchasing women-owned services and products, making connections between female entrepreneurs who have synergy, collaborating with a women-owned business, hosting an event around female entrepreneurship, or gifting items from women-owned businesses to others. It's associations like WO3 that have helped me expand my mindset so I could get out of the comfort and safety zone and into the growth and prosperity zone.

FACE TO FACE WITH UNWORTHINESS

It was not until I faced unworthiness head on in my first marriage that I realized it was possible to truly overcome a self-limiting belief and that playing it safe would never allow me to feel truly fulfilled. I got married at twenty-two years old—right out of college—to my high school sweetheart, who I was in a relationship with for seven years. In fact, I graduated from college, got married, and started working at my consulting firm in the same month back in June of 2005. That was an immense amount of change at once. My daily routine, livelihood, and relationships would completely change in a matter of days. When my marriage did not work out and I got divorced three years later, unworthiness hit me like a ton of bricks. I felt like I was drowning. I did not feel worthy of a long-term relationship and maybe not even real love—just like I was not worthy of jobs that I perceived were too big for me. After all, my mom lost my dad and never remarried, so I should just accept once again, "this must be as good as it gets." I figured out (which took much longer than I would have liked), that this limited thinking was flat out garbage. I gave into a limiting belief that was simply untrue.

At twenty-five years old, I dove into a deeper self-development journey, one I am still on today. I've always read self-development books, but it was not until I was faced with the most arduous of adversities that I had to apply tools that I began to acquire. It was this time of my life when adaptability took on a whole new meaning for me. I adapted to new ways of thinking, problem-solving, and engaging with the world around me. One of the books I will never forget receiving is *Eat, Pray, Love* by Elizabeth Gilbert, which was released the year before my divorce in 2007. I was ashamed to reveal to a female leader at work that I was struggling through a divorce. I was afraid of judgement in the workplace and worried people may think I wouldn't be able to maintain appropriate focus on my clients and responsibilities. To my surprise, the leader I confided in didn't judge me. She listened intently at one of the darkest times of my life and sent along Gilbert's book to my home. The book changed my perspective on starting over, rediscovering and connecting to myself, choosing spontaneity and adventure, and embracing the present moment. I enjoyed watching the movie version of the book released in 2010 starring Julia Roberts. I was in the height of singlehood at the time, and I appreciated the profound experience of going from adversity to adventure.

As difficult as it may feel, especially when you're in the thick of adversity, it is in the times of greatest challenge that we experience the greatest growth. Getting divorced for me meant starting over—not just the logistical tasks of finding a new place to live and getting a new car but re-establishing a new and reinvigorated sense of self. Imagine your identity tied to someone else for a decade, and then finding that in your mid-twenties, you are reinventing yourself. That was my life. The growth of reconnecting to myself was incredible. I discovered what made me feel alive; traveled; deepened my friendships; and worked on my healing journey through therapy, reading, journaling, self-development events, and experiencing new adventures—especially in the fitness space like Tough Mudder, Civilian Military Combine, and half marathons. Being single was the best thing that could have ever happened to me at the time. I found *me*.

Reinvention is something that helps us continuously grow through our self-limiting beliefs. We reinvent ourselves often and don't even realize it. With major life experiences—a career change, new relationship, trauma, new baby, move, sabbatical, travel adventure—comes an expanded lens of the world and therefore a piece of reinvention within. These experiences drive behavior change and encourage us to challenge our outlook on the world.

Embrace that change. It's like turning on the panoramic view of your camera. When you expand your view, you see and experience the world in a way that you haven't before. Expanding is the opposite of limiting. When I was in a state of expansion, the notion of unworthiness began to dissipate for me. When you find yourself in the space of limitation, turn on your panoramic vision and think to yourself, *What can I do to expand my perspective in this moment?*

I also learned through reinvention how impactful it is to let go of labels. The author and TED Talk speaker, Dr. Amanda Foo-Ryland, who I talk more about later in the book, helped me recognize the freedom you attain when you adopt label-less living. Labels box us into categories, which are limiting and can have negative connotations attached to them. For example, being divorced doesn't mean I have to introduce myself as a divorcee. I just happened to be a person who has gone through the experience of divorce, but the event doesn't define who I am as a person, nor does it limit me from future relationships. Recently, I interviewed Steven Cohen, the co-founder of Sunder Energy. He was a college dropout and today, he's a millennial millionaire. If he let the label of "dropout" define him, he may not have gone on to build a solar empire. Amanda is *Amanda*. Steven is *Steven*. I am *Dez*. You are *you*. That makes us each unique. Let go of labels. You are who you choose to be despite your past or what others want for you. Finding *you* and owning who you are begins with radical self-awareness.

RADICAL SELF-AWARENESS

Through my own personal experience and exploration of self-limiting beliefs, I have learned that overcoming your self-limiting beliefs starts with radical self-awareness. You see, limiting beliefs begin with the self, but they can also be conquered by the self. That is just it, they are self-imposed! These limiting beliefs come from our past, upbringing, what people have said to us, negative experiences we have faced, and the environments that influence us. Radical self-awareness is about taking stock of who you are in each dimension of your life. Think about a pie with eight to ten slices. Each of those slices represent major areas such as (but are not limited to): love relationships, friendships, health/wellness, finances, social/recreation, spirituality, personal growth, career, learning, skills, creative life, family, community/service. Jot down the areas that are most important to you. Then rate each on a scale of one through ten with one meaning needs substantial improvement and ten meaning stellar. When you are radically self-aware, you have a strong sense of where you are in life, what you want to work on, and how you want to evolve. Don't feel bad for anything less than a ten. In fact, it'd be surprising if anything was a ten. Perfect is not a goal to strive for here. The objective is being real and honest with yourself so you can expend your energy where you want to grow. Growth is incremental, so don't beat yourself for not making every stride a massive one. Progress is more important than perfection.

Through two decades (and counting) of inner work and research of how the 150-plus guests on my podcast have overcome self-limiting beliefs, I have developed a simple, five-step approach called A5 (Assess, Analyze, Adjust, Act, Align) that will help you overcome your self-limiting beliefs. The pages ahead of you will unlock these steps as well as examples from myself and others that illustrate a limitless life awaits you. My brand is called Born Unbreakable because I believe that every single one of us has an unbreakable spirit. When you step into an unbreakable mindset, you manifest abundance and become more unapologetic about who you are, what you stand for, and how you want to show up in the world.

Overcoming your self-limiting beliefs is an inside-out process, meaning that it starts from within. The keys to sustainment are two-dimensional, internal, and external. The internal relates to your purpose, your mindset, and your habits. The external relates to your inputs (what you feed your mind, body, and soul) and your influences (who and what you let shape your perspective).

Remember that pie chart I talked about earlier? How you treat those dimensions of your life impacts both the internal and external. I've had internal and external devils and demons to reckon with, which is the backbone of why writing this book is so important to me: I don't want those devils and demons to win in my life—or yours. I've encountered stories of friends, loved ones, clients, and even strangers I've connected with throughout my travels about feeling limited. I know firsthand how debilitating a self-limiting belief can be. A self-limiting belief can have the power of robbing people from achieving their dreams, pursuing their aspirations, and simply having hope for a better and more fulfilling life. Limiting beliefs only have power if we let them.

It's my devotion to help others live a limitless life. My hope for you in reading this book is that you walk away embracing and expressing exactly who you are, and that you have a new framework to apply any time a self-limiting belief knocks on your window and tries to bully its way into your driver's seat. Tune out those voices that don't serve you and listen to the voices that do. You are your only limit and starting today, you will take new action to break down your self-limiting beliefs, expand your outlook, and embrace all the things that make you, YOU.

2

THE ORIGINS OF OUR LIMITATIONS

THE *BORN UNBREAKABLE PODCAST SHOW* has become my graduate-level education. There are people who pursue advanced degrees in subjects like law, medicine, or business. Then there are the divergent who pursue the road less traveled, or maybe just the road bumpier and more unknown like me. I devote hours regularly to interviewing some of the brightest, most creative, innovative, courageous, and astounding individuals on the planet. The time I spend doing this isn't a job; it's a passion. It is like attending a school for life. Instead of asking professors questions in a large class setting, I ask brilliant minds questions in a one-on-one setting, and the lessons I have learned are priceless. I do not write term papers or take exams, which is certainly a bonus, but I learn major life lessons and apply them day after day—everything from changing my morning routine and how I set goals to the way I approach relationships and business; taking real-time action is the most valuable homework assignment I have ever done.

The guests who come on my show are not only people that I learn from, but often people that I become friends with. It is from their stories and experiences that the A5 method I have developed was born. Before I break down each step of the A5 (Assess, Analyze, Adjust, Act, Align) methodology, it is vital that I spend time discussing further the common origins of our limitations. It is when we understand why we limit ourselves that we can overcome our limitations. The inward journey sparks the epiphanies or lightbulb moments that illuminate new paths.

PAIN AND TRAUMA

Let us start with the familiar origin of our past pain or trauma. Our past can be both a blessing and a curse. A series of positive experiences tends to lend itself to an outlook that is positive. Conversely, a past with notable trauma can color the lens by which we view and experience the world in a negative way. In Episode 26 of my podcast show, I interviewed a beautiful soul named Gavin McCoy. Gavin's story begins with his mother who grew up in Ireland. She moved from convent to convent and eventually lived with a foster family on a farm where she was repeatedly beaten and raped. Gavin was born in England where his mother eventually moved. Sadly, as a young boy Gavin experienced abuse and witnessed his mother in a cycle of unhealthy relationships. This trauma led to Gavin turning to drugs and alcohol. One of his self-limiting beliefs was that everyone thought he was crazy. Gavin shares that it was countless hours of counseling, therapy, group discussions, introspection, and journaling that helped him persevere. It was also the identity work that he did that helped him discover his biological roots.

Today, Gavin is an identity coach who helps people have a better understanding of where they've come from, specifically men who have experienced abuse and those who want to find their biological families. As I heard the renowned branding strategist and co-founder of Brand Builders Group Rory Vaden say on stage at the Summit of Greatness 2022, "You are best positioned to serve the person that you once were." Gavin is a living example. He understands his past but no longer lets it define him. He's positioned himself to help those who suffer the same experiences he once did. Gavin is a resounding case of turning pain into purpose and power.

THE LOW POINTS OF LIFE

Limited thinking can also be born from the low points in our lives, not necessarily a traumatic upbringing, but a series of unique moments that create a repository. If you have ever seen the movie *Inside Out*, each time the main character, an eleven-year-old girl named Riley, had an experience, assorted colored memory orbs would form. The colors represented moments of joy, sadness, anger, fear, or disgust. The collection of traumatic memories forms a repository that can make us question our power and capabilities, in particular the events that have emotional significance. In the movie, the memory orbs funnel through vacuum tubes, and the long-term memories are stored in a library of endless shelves. Patterns and trends (particularly those that are less than ideal) can set a tone for what someone expects because they assume they're destined for more of the same. If you were born into poverty and an environment where limitations were a way of life, you may believe financial success is impossible. If heartbreak is the result of every meaningful relationship you've ever had, you may believe that future relationships will result similarly. If studying and getting good grades was difficult for you in school, you may think that you're not smart enough to attain the career or achieve the goals you desire. If obesity runs in the family, you may believe that you too are destined for obesity. These statements can be true, but they certainly don't have to be. We are not defined by our past or the choices of others. Who you are and who you want to be are based on what you believe to be true for your life. Does this sound like a repeat statement? It is and I repeat myself with intention. I can't stress enough how important it is not to give away your power by letting others dictate the outcomes in your life.

In Episode 52, I interviewed a wonderful woman named LisaBeth Thomas. One of LisaBeth's self-limiting beliefs was that she was not good enough. As unbelievable as this may sound, LisaBeth lost her marriage, her home, her business, and then her mother. This series of devastating events completely crushed her confidence. If you lost everything that you felt made you whole, what would you do? What LisaBeth did initially was look for validation from others to get empathy for her sorrows, but as she went deeper into her reflection, she began to accept her reality and take responsibility for the role that she played in each event that did not go the way she wanted. There were things she could not control, but there were also things she could control. She recognized her pattern of avoidance and in her words, began to "trip over everything she swept under the rug." It is when she took responsibility for her life and faced the fears that caused her patterns of limitations that she learned how to be triumphant. As a speaker, producer, and marketing expert today, she helps people face their fears and prevail beyond them. LisaBeth figured out that the only way to move past the devastation she experienced was to be radically self-aware of her tendencies so she could start to create different outcomes.

OTHER PEOPLE'S JOURNEYS

A sneaky source of limited thinking is comparison to the journey of other people. This is exacerbated by the information age we live in—television, radio, podcasts, YouTube, newspapers, articles, social media, blogs, and the overall world-wide web. I say sneaky because while we go to information sources for knowledge, inspiration, or clarification, we can leave those sources with envy, self-doubt, or disappointment by comparing ourselves to the lives of others and questioning why our progress or results are not the same as theirs. There are other people who are richer, smarter, farther along, younger, more skilled, more traveled, more advantaged, more connected, and more revered. This kind of limited thinking leads to self-sabotage.

Self-sabotage is basing your journey on someone else's blueprint. The only person you should be comparing yourself to is *you*. Are you better than you were last year, last month, and yesterday? I do understand that it is natural to examine the world around you, so if you do find yourself looking at other people's journeys, look for inspiration and motivation. The positive framing will help you grow instead of feeling stifled. When I went to a self-development workshop on business marketing a few years ago, one of the facilitators shared a visual that stuck with me. He drew a picture depicting "you" on a flip chart. He illustrated arrows in front and behind you. He pointed out how there will always be people in front of you that you can learn from and people behind you that can learn from you. Instead of placing so much weight on what others have accomplished or attained that you haven't, look at their experiences as ones you can learn from. You have the power of prevailing by taking a limited way of thinking and flipping it into encouragement and motivation.

After I became a certified coach and started taking private coaching clients, I was riddled with comparative, self-sabotaging thoughts. I saw the life of coaches and influencer-types like Lewis Howes, Ed Mylett, Rachel Hollis, Mel Robbins, and Jay Shetty and thought, "Holy crap, how can I ever reach the number of people that they do?" I had to realize what matters is that I reach people one at a time in my own unique way, not the same way these other people do. Each of us has the advantage of our own unique experiences and stories that will find connection with the people they're meant to reach. The other thing to remember is that when you're collecting information or observing someone else's life, especially when you're observing from afar, you are not equipped with a complete picture. What you see is a snapshot in time or a highlight reel of what they want you to see. Everyone is working on their own lives, so you don't need to spend time on them; give that energy to your own life, the only one you have control over.

OTHER PEOPLE'S OPINIONS

There is another source of limitation. It is my favorite one to unpack. It may very well be the most difficult source because it is the most inhibitive to unleashing your true potential. I call this limited thinking *living life on other peo-*

ple's terms. The best way I have seen this framed is by the author Bronnie Ware, who wrote *The Top Five Regrets of the Dying: A Life Transformed by the Dearly Departing.* The book is published in thirty-two languages. Bronnie worked in palliative care for many years. She asked her patients about their regrets and what they would do differently, and she gathered common themes. She writes about the top five themes in her international best-selling book. Do you want to take a guess at what the number-one theme was? "I wish I'd had the courage to live a life true to myself, not the one others expected of me."

Wow, learning that data point was a wake-up call. I spent most of my life trying to live up to everyone else's expectations and therefore, suffered in silence and solitude. I firmly believe that when you spend time getting to intimately know yourself and decide to live life on your own terms versus the terms of someone else, you open the door to untapped potential. You also will not worry about who does not accept you. When you can be authentically you, the right people will rally around you and appreciate your uniqueness. There is far greater value in the quality over the quantity of people in your life. The people who do not believe in you, doubt you, or constantly have a negative opinion are merely spectators. You can go so far as to exercise boundaries and put them on the not invited list.

What about the example from the hit 2023 summer movie *Barbie* starring Margot Robbie as Barbie and Ryan

Gosling as Ken? The duo goes on a self-discovery journey after Barbie starts malfunctioning. Her perfect appearance and perfect life start going haywire, and she goes on a quest to figure out why. A major theme in the movie, in addition to self-acceptance and idealized femininity, is unrealistic expectations. The character Gloria, played by actress America Ferrera, is a Mattel employee who has a famous monologue. The monologue serves as a critical turning point in the movie where Barbie begins to accept that perfectionism is an impossible standard. Here is the inspiring monologue:

> *It is literally impossible to be a woman. You are so beautiful and so smart, and it kills me that you don't think you're good enough. Like, we have to always be extraordinary, but somehow we're always doing it wrong. You have to be thin, but not too thin. And you can never say you want to be thin. You have to say you want to be healthy, but also you have to be thin. You have to have money, but you can't ask for money because that's crass. You have to be a boss, but you can't be mean. You have to lead, but you can't squash other people's ideas. You're supposed to love being a mother but don't talk about your kids all the damn time. You have to be a career woman*

but also always be looking out for other peo-
ple. You have to answer for men's bad behav-
ior, which is insane, but if you point that
out, you're accused of complaining. You're
supposed to stay pretty for men, but not so
pretty that you tempt them too much or that
you threaten other women because you're
supposed to be a part of the sisterhood. But
always stand out and always be grateful. But
never forget that the system is rigged. So find
a way to acknowledge that but also always be
grateful. You have to never get old, never be
rude, never show off, never be selfish, never
fall down, never fail, never show fear, never
get out of line. It's too hard! It's too contra-
dictory and nobody gives you a medal or says
thank you! And it turns out in fact that not
only are you doing everything wrong, but
also everything is your fault.

Gloria's monologue perfectly summarizes the societal conundrum we live in. Unreasonable expectations
are placed on many groups of people, and each day these
groups around the globe are striving to live up to them.
Outrageous standards wreak havoc on our overall psychology and mental stability because they are impractical to
meet. These expectations are merely popularized opinions

that get shoved down our throats through every medium that reaches human eyes and ears. So often, we fight to fit in which puts us in a fight with our authenticity.

In Episode 71, I interviewed my now friend, Kelly Calia, also known as Kel Cal. Kel too suffered by trying to live up to other people's expectations of her. Just like LisaBeth, Kel was plagued by the self-limiting belief that she was not enough. She had what appeared to be the socially acceptable standard of a dream life. She lived in sunny South Florida in a big, beautiful, paid-off home, drove a Porsche, and had four goldendoodle dogs. Kel and her husband were successful real estate agents and business partners. They were financially well-off. Outsiders looking in would admire or even envy the life Kel had. What people did not see was how badly Kel suffered on the inside. She was in an emotionally abusive marriage. She made the courageous decision to leave her marriage and start over in Seattle where her sister lived. She went on a deep self-discovery journey, and her self-awareness skyrocketed. She experienced radical self-awareness by exploring the things that filled her up with joy inside and expanding her perspective to realize the limitations she was placing on herself. Her healing journey is what led Kel to starting her brand, How I Cured My Resting Bitch Face, and launching her podcast, *Dear Dumb Bitch*.

As the legend of podcasting, John Lee Dumas, once said when I heard him speak at an event called Rise &

Record in Fall of 2022, "your message is in your mess," and "the reality is that people want to be inspired by others who they can see in themselves." Kel's mess is absolutely her message. Today, her confidence is greater than it has ever been, and she made the decision to leave real estate to devote her energy full-time to helping women get out of toxic relationships. She is now living her passion from Bali, Indonesia and completed writing her first book. I'm excited to share that Kel launched her book, *How I Cured My Resting Bitch Face: Your Guide to Stop Settling, Fall in Love with Yourself, & Create a Life You're Obsessed With*, in March 2024. It is available for purchase now, so look it up online. Kel's journey inspires me every day, and I feel blessed that our paths crossed. One of the special experiences we got to share is Kel visiting Las Vegas for the first time and recording me on her podcast as her first guest. Check out Episode 83 of my podcast show, and you can hear Kel interview me. Follow her on Instagram @iamkelcal, and you can be inspired by her too.

CULTURAL NORMS

The norms influenced by the cultures we grew up in can perpetuate limited beliefs subconsciously. Jo Koy is a Filipino American comedian who I enjoy watching. I can relate to his comedy because he jokes about the Filipino culture which I was raised in. He jokes about the most common professions that Filipinos choose in America, which are in the fields of nursing and postal services. In a comedic setting, joking about these professions does make me laugh because the statistics do show that many Filipinos choose to become nurses or postal workers. These are great professions; however, they are not the only professions Filipinos can choose, and certainly Filipinos shouldn't feel limited to these choices merely because it's what other Filipinos choose.

In a previous relationship, my partner grew up in Mexico. Cultural norms that came up in our conversations were how many women did the domestic work at home while men were the breadwinners. Another topic in our relationship was around therapy and how men growing up in traditional Mexican culture don't believe in going to therapy. These norms were in direct opposition to my beliefs, which are that women can have wildly successful careers and don't always play a domesticated role in the home, and that therapy can be for everyone if they so choose to partake. Many cultures have histories, stereotypes, and traditions of patterns and behaviors which can be limiting. These are perpetuated by TV shows, movies, music, news, and social media. Can you think of limitations perpetuated by cultures that you've been associated with or exposed to? Have you caught yourself in limited thinking because of traditional cultural narratives? The decisions that you make today can shift the course of history by writing a new narrative that can influence the generations of tomorrow.

THE LIFE CYCLE OF SELF-LIMITING BELIEFS

The below picture helps to illustrate the self-limiting belief cycle that we go through over time. This is a depiction of two major life events that broke my faith and led me to no longer believe in myself and my worthiness. The A5 (Assess, Analyze, Adjust, Act, Align) process you will learn about in this book is designed to get you moving back in the direction of faith over fear so you can choose hope over helplessness. You may have been bruised more than once in your life, but you are never beyond repair. You can have hope and you can heal.

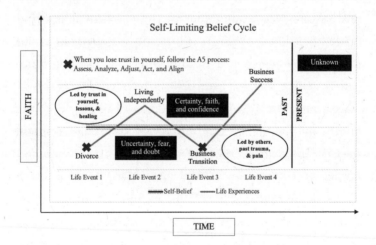

As we look at this diagram, it illustrates that there are points in life that may make us fearful and doubtful like trauma (e.g., divorce and business transition). There are other experiences that make us feel confident (e.g., living independently and business success). Below the Self-Belief line (low points), in a state of fearfulness, we may be more influenced by the opinions of others and emotions like pain and sorrow. Above the Self-Belief line (high points), our inclination is to trust more in ourselves, our lessons, and the healing journey. The A5 (Assess, Analyze, Adjust, Act, Align) process helps us to navigate more quickly to a state of faith and confidence over fear and doubt.

It is important for me to share that this self-limiting belief cycle is something that we all experience as human beings although I understand that it may feel like you are alone suffering in silence. You do not have to go through any agonizing experience on your own. It is through community and human connection that we grow from the painful experiences and adversities we have had. When I was at the Teleos Leadership Institute in Pennsylvia to work on becoming a certified coach by the International Coach Federation in 2016, group activities were an integral part of the leadership development program and our learning process. In the small group I was put in, one of the activities we had to do was draw a timeline of our lives on a big sheet of white flip-chart paper. The timeline was a more extensive picture of the visual that I shared with you above. We were tasked to draw out all the high and low points in our lives and present them to our small groups one at a time. I presented mine first because I wanted to get it over with. I was terrified that I would be judged because one of the low points I wrote about was divorce. After everyone in my group presented, I learned that each person had either gone through one or more divorces. The one event in my life that I was ashamed of and afraid that I would be judged for was something *everyone* in the room had experienced.

So, never assume that you are the only one who has gone through the things that you have. You never know if the person that you are sitting or standing next to has gone through the exact same thing. We have more commonalities that you might think. Another powerful lesson I learned through my coaching certification program is that what we fear others are judging us for are just projections of our own thoughts and worries. We can sometimes project the judgments that we have about ourselves onto others when their perception of us could be completely different. You are your own worst critic, not other people. The lessons I talk about will remind you to give yourself grace. This isn't the first time you'll hear me say this. You're human. Humans are imperfect and will make mistakes. It's normal. When it comes to your self-limiting beliefs, know that you don't just have to go through it, but you will absolutely grow through it. Stick with me—you will see!

3

FROM BREAK-UP TO BREAKTHROUGH

IT IS THE SUMMER OF 2019, July 9 to be exact. I was sitting with a good friend by the pool of our girlfriend's house in Brentwood, California. Podcasts were a big part of our daily learning. I had the brilliant idea of starting a podcast myself or better yet, starting one with my friend. I talked through the idea aloud, and my friend loved it. We both were enthusiastic about helping others. We wanted to help women over thirty stop putting themselves last. I was a multicultural woman in my thirties, and she was a Caucasian woman in her fifties. I was progressive, and she was conservative. She had eight kids, and I had none. She devoted her life to being a homemaker, and I devoted my life to my consulting career. Despite our different worlds, we thought how cool it would be for two unique women who found friendship in our struggles—we were both overcoming heartbreak—to come together and help other women who also needed to reconnect with their joy, self-worth, and confidence. We got so excited that we started brainstorming names for the podcast. At the time, we thought *Manifest Quest* was a good title, and we started envisioning what a podcast cover would look like. There was one problem though: we had no earthly clue how to start a podcast!

One of the podcasts I listened to daily was *The School of Greatness* hosted by Lewis Howes, a former professional American handball player and lifestyle entrepreneur. His mission was and still is to help others overcome self-doubt. I learned that he hosts an in-person event every September called The Summit of Greatness. Besides the inspiration I knew I would experience at the event, I figured there must be smart people at this event who know a thing or two about starting a podcast, so I decided to attend. I walked out of the gym one day and told my friend over the phone that I was attending the event (which was only two weeks away), and she could not stand the idea of not going, so she committed to attending with me. That decision changed both of our lives forever.

THE BIRTH OF BLISSFUL FORTITUDE

The Summit of Greatness was a three-day event held in Columbus, Ohio the first weekend after Labor Day. Our excitement was undying. Every moment of our adventure to, during, and from our trip to Columbus was documented. I now wonder what the people sitting next to us on the plane were thinking when we were enthusiastically brainstorming about our vision of becoming a dynamic duo of podcast hosts who would help countless women all over the world. I am going to pretend they were inspired and not annoyed. We met the most remarkable individuals at the event—creatives, healers, change-makers, and game changers.

One of the people we met in the elevator of our hotel on the way to the event one morning was April Garcia. We did not know it at the time, but it turned out that April is an international business advisor, performance coach, speaker on strategy and mindset, host of the *PivotMe* podcast, and all-around Certified Bad Ass (she also wrote the foreword of this book). April became one of our magnificent event buddies, but beyond that she connected us to her podcast manager Ben Williams (the brilliant founder of Rokkwood Audio, where they specialize in podcasts, music and production, and audio branding) who soon enough became our podcast manager. April also connected us to Brand Builders Group, who we ended up partnering with to develop our brand and our podcast approach. Within twenty-one days, we had a team of experts who were going to help us make our podcasting dreams come true.

In the Fall of 2019, Blissful Fortitude the brand and *Bliss Beyond F.E.A.R. (Faith, Elevate, Action, Results)* the podcast was born. We had a daily devotion to our new endeavor. We scheduled quarterly photoshoots. We launched our website and social media pages. We hired a virtual assistant to manage our social media campaigns. We developed and recorded a confidence course for women. We began discussing what our first book would be and what launch would look like. We talked about pricing packages for coaching programs. We quickly started recording episodes and decided that January 11, 2020 would be our debut launch party for our podcast where guests would get to hear several episodes we released at the beginning of the new year. Over two hundred people attended our podcast launch party, including our sensational elevator buddy, April, who helped catapult our new adventure. It was surreal. Seeing our friends and family all in one room celebrating our new venture with us was exhilarating.

THE BREAK-UP

My friend and I released sixty-nine episodes of *Bliss Beyond F.E.A.R.*, and it was one of the greatest learning experiences of my life. The format of our show was addressing questions that people submitted to us or doing interviews of those who aligned with our mission. I experienced a tremendous deal of tenacity, resilience, courage, and growth. Episode 69 was the announcement of our "break-up." It was unexpected. For over a year, we poured our hearts and souls into growing our podcast, developing our coaching program and curriculum, and exploring how to write our first book together. Everywhere we went, Blissful Fortitude was the first thing we talked about with people. It was a part of our identity. After starting a new relationship and re-evaluating her priorities, she was compelled to make the difficult decision to walk away from our partnership. Now, identity reinvention was upon us both. All the hours we devoted to Blissful Fortitude were no more. We both had to make decisions about where to dedicate our time.

Shortly after my friend revealed her new path, I heard, "Knock, knock!" and said, "Who is there?" A reply screamed, "It's me, your friend, Unworthiness; I'd like to take you for another ride." There was that darn self-limiting belief...*again!* This time it had invited itself into my world because the original plan I envisioned was blown to bits. I thought we were going to build a coaching business, write a book, and do a podcast *as a team*. Was I capable of going at this whole thing on my own? The fear of failure crept in. There are so many solopreneurs in the self-development space. Being a dynamic duo is what would make us stand apart from the rest.

I was at a crossroads. I could give up the dream of impacting millions of people, or I could find the belief in myself that I was worthy and capable of building an inspirational brand that would genuinely represent me and speak to the heart of others. To figure out my next move, I went to the one place that helped me find answers before, the same place that I went when I was twenty-five years old rebuilding the pieces of my life after divorce…inward. Admittedly, I was also thinking of the pity party scene from the comedy movie *Bridesmaids* (2011) when Megan says to Annie after feeling sorry for herself for all the things going wrong in her life, "You're your problem, Annie, and you're also your solution." I turned to comedic relief because I wanted to avoid thinking about my troubling situation. There is a common denominator at every difficult decision or crossroads you've ever faced in your life: YOU. You are always present at the scene. Therefore, you hold the power to decide what's next.

THE SHOW MUST GO ON

I discovered a few things as I reflected on what the next chapter of my journey would be like. First, I thought, "Break-ups suck." It was a very real but unproductive thought, so I next reflected on my "why." What was my purpose for building out a motivational brand that would offer coaching, a podcast, and training programs? My why was to help inspire people to live their best, most abundant life. With Blissful Fortitude, the mission was to specifically help women embrace their worth and find their joy. Now I needed to think about what that would look like in my solo adventure. Next, I reflected on what resources I would need to successfully rebrand. A terrific book that helped me think through this was *Who Not How: The Formula to Achieve Bigger Goals Through Accelerating Teamwork* by Dan Sullivan and Benjamin Hardy. I highly recommend this book if you want to gain more leverage in your entrepreneurial journey. Lastly, I remembered a quote by the famous former quarterback of the Tampa Bay Buccaneers (and before that the New England Patriots), Tom Brady: "I didn't come this far to only come this far."

If there is one thing that I have learned by watching the most successful people on the planet, it is that they take action even when they do not have all the answers. Greatness is more about will than skill. One of my favorite examples is Oprah Winfrey. She happens to be an Aquarius just like me, born nine days after my birthday on January 29. We have in common being natural-born go-getters. Oprah was born into poverty in rural Mississippi to a single teenage mother. She was molested in her youth and got pregnant but lost her son in infancy. The odds were stacked against her based on how she grew up, but she had an unyielding will to create a better life for herself. Her skills in broadcasting and hosting came later through her years of dedication. If Oprah could persevere, particularly in such challenging circumstances, I sure could. So, after I reflected on the break-up with my business partner, I swiftly moved into action. When I say swift, I mean that I started a new brand and launched my solo podcast two weeks after releasing my last episode of *Bliss Beyond F.E.A.R.* When you want something bad enough, and if you are clear on why, you will figure out how.

BORN UNBREAKABLE

I started by connecting with the right "who." My who was my best friend, confidant, and trusted business partner today, Aaron. Together, we are the epitome of a dream team; we are incredibly aligned personally and professionally. The best part is that we have the exact opposite skill sets. He is phenomenal at absolutely everything I am not—all things creative, audio, visual, technical, and marketing. All the things that are required to start a brand and a podcast were directly in Aaron's wheelhouse. We strategized daily. I cooked up the name Born Unbreakable at two o'clock in the morning one day. I made a list of forty-eight potential names, and Born Unbreakable was number forty-six. The message I wanted to share with the world was undeniably clear: *Be Unapologetically You.* Aaron designed my powerful logo, and that is why you see the B and the U stand out in Born Unbreakable; my message shows up in my brand name. Aaron also designed my website overnight: https://bornunbreakable.com. Note that while writing this book, Aaron has become a co-host of the *Born Unbreakable* podcast, so you'll want to tune in because the caliber of the podcast has undeniably been elevated by adding another perspective.

The exercise of starting over allowed me to take a step back and truly assess what success looked like. A huge part of that was the recognition that achieving greatness is not a solo act. Having the right partner and/or team is paramount. You see, sometimes a setback can allow you to make a comeback. Recalibrating helped me to understand what didn't work in my previous partnership and what was required to make a new partnership thrive. While my first partner and I shared similar ideas and short-term goals, our longer-term vision and intentions were different. I found that what I needed in a sustainable partnership was an aligned mindset, complementary skills, a shared vision, a similar work ethic, and the desire to play the long game. With an aligned team, there are no limits to what you can accomplish.

I immediately started recording episodes, and of course my first guest had to be none other than the woman I bumped into in the elevator at the Summit of Greatness in September of 2019: April Garcia. Today, April is a dear friend and mentor. I participated in her life-changing *PivotMe* mastermind for three years. Aaron and I filmed my launch trailer, and the podcast went live on April 21, 2021, on all major podcast platforms and YouTube. I took the list of everything I wanted to do with my previous brand and podcast and made it a reality with Born Unbreakable. I was grateful for the gift of experience. I embraced the belief that when one good thing ends, an even better thing can be born. Two weeks of sleepless nights was worth every single second. By eighteen months, I recorded double the number of podcast episodes that I did in the year I was a part of Blissful Fortitude. I have realized that being tested brings us our most compelling testimonies. I'm reminded of a quote I once saw: "Not all storms come to disrupt your life, some come to clear your path." This break-up ended up becoming my breakthrough.

4

THE PATH TO OVERCOMING
YOUR SELF-LIMITING BELIEFS

NOW THAT YOU HAVE A foundation for what a self-limiting belief is, and how they hold us back, the obvious question is, how do you crush your self-limiting beliefs? A5 (Assess, Analyze, Adjust, Act, Align) is the path I am inviting you to walk on today. The thread that weaves my guests from all over the world together is not just that they have experienced self-limiting beliefs, it is also that they were born unbreakable by demonstrating resilience and willingness to get out of their own way. That is what A5 is all about, shifting the way you think and behave. One of my favorite sayings comes from Gandhi: "Your beliefs become your thoughts; your thoughts become your words; your words become your actions; your actions become your habits; your habits become your values; your values become your destiny."

YOUR COMPASS

There are five foundational elements to filter through each step of the A5 (Assess, Analyze, Adjust, Act, Align) process: purpose, mindset, habits, inputs, and influences. These elements comprise your essence. Imagine these elements as your personal life compass. Like the foundation of a house, the compass is a depiction of standing on solid, stable ground. Purpose is in the center to remind you of your core, who you are, what you stand for, and what motivates you daily. On each directional spoke are the other four elements. Your compass will help guide you in the direction that needs attention, and that will constantly change.

MINDSET

INPUTS   PURPOSE   HABITS

INFLUENCES

Purpose is what gets you out of bed every morning and what you reflect on when you lay your head down at night. What is your mission? What is the legacy that you want to leave behind?

Mindset is the foundational operating system of how you think. Do your thoughts tend to be fixed and scarcity focused on what you lack? Or are you growth focused on how you can live abundantly and thrive?

Habits are the subconscious behaviors that you do daily. Beyond what you think, habits are how you show up in the world. What is your daily routine? What are the things you do consistently?

Inputs are what you feed your mind, body, and spirit. What do you consume? What are you reading, watching, and listening to? What are you eating and drinking?

Influences are who and what you let into your environment. What kind of space do you live and work in? An entrepreneur, Jim Rohn would ask, "Who are the five people you spend the most time with?"

THE A5 METHODOLOGY

The five steps of the A5 process are: Assess, Analyze, Adjust, Act, Align. This framework will redefine how you manage self-limiting beliefs that emerge in times of change, instability, difficulty, uncertainty, transition, and even opportunity.

Assess is about being a big picture observer of your life. It is starting where your feet are and acknowledging the present. Where are you right now in life and where do you want to be? What problem or obstacle are you trying to solve?

Analyze is understanding how you got to where you are and what steps you are going to take to get to your next destination. What is the data in your life telling you? What is working and what is not working?

Adjust is realizing what small shifts are required to achieve the outcomes that you desire. What do you observe must be done differently? What are you willing to change or try?

Act is taking intentional steps to evoke improvement. What new thoughts and behaviors are you adopting? How are you tracking progress? What are you doing to stay accountable to your new habits?

Align is tying your small steps back to your why. What is your goal and how are the actions you are taking aligned with the vision you have for your life? What does sustainability look like?

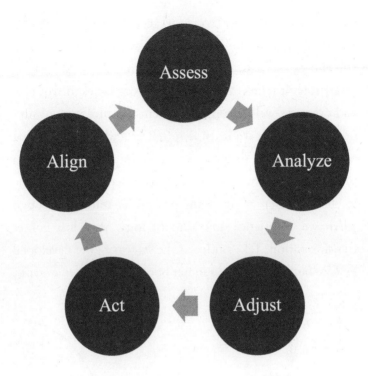

THE STAGES OF GRIEF

To walk on this journey, it requires you to go where everyone discussed in this book so far has gone: within. It is within us where the greatest magic is unleashed. When my business partnership ended, identity coach Gavin's addictions became unbearable, marketing whiz LisaBeth's losses crushed her spirit, and realtor Kel's marriage was crumbling, the resolutions we sought were within us. A conscious decision needed to be made for each of us to feel, heal, learn, and grow. Allow yourself to feel every emotion that emerges. Don't run away from those feelings. Avoidance is commonly easier than acceptance, but when you choose avoidance, the battle within still brews. Healing takes time. It requires the process of forgiveness of yourself and others as well as support, potentially professional support like therapy. To learn is to reflect and recognize what better looks like. To grow is to take intentional action in the direction of improvement. It takes dedicated discipline to change. There is a grieving process we must go through when we experience any kind of loss. After loss comes transformation. Take notice of the stages of grief developed by Elisabeth Kübler-Ross in her book *On Death and Dying.*

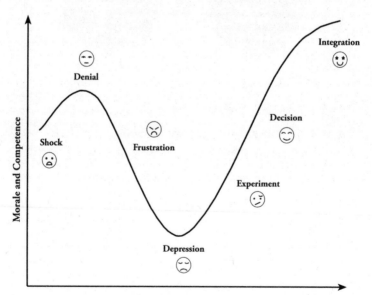

Here's how she defines each stage:

Shock: surprise or shock at the event

Denial: disbelief; looking for evidence that it isn't true

Frustration: recognition that things are different; sometimes angry

Depression: low mood; lacking in energy

Experiment: initial engagement with the new situation

Decision: learning how to work in the new situation; feeling more positive

Integration: changes integrated; a renewed individual

When I became certified as a change management expert, this is one of the concepts I spent time studying. The more times we go on the rollercoaster of grief, the more resilient we become because as we begin to see and experience new losses or changes, our path to accelerating our breakthroughs becomes faster. Our ability to gain self-awareness is sharper. The tools we are equipped with are more abundant.

I will go back to the two examples of unworthiness I talked about earlier to illustrate how my acceleration curve changed. When I was twenty-five years old and experiencing divorce, I was unequipped for the kind of loss I was going through. It was difficult for me to cope and process the level of change and depth of pain I was going through. Every stage of grief felt like an eternity. After I learned about my then-husband's infidelity, it took me four months to decide that I wanted to leave my ten-year relationship. In hindsight, I am impressed that it was only months and not years. I did not have the emotional wherewithal at the time to know how to deal with my situation. At that point in my life, avenues like therapy were foreign to me. However, it took me three years to get back on my feet independently again. I begrudgingly took what I thought was a step back by moving back in with my mom at the age of twenty-five. I was embarrassed and ashamed and felt like a complete failure. I spent seven years from eighteen to twenty-five working on becoming independent only to return home. At twenty-eight years old, I bought my own place and finally felt like I was on a new trajectory. I allowed myself to go through my grief, and it took years to heal, learn, and grow. As the famous poet Maya Angelou once said, "Do the best you can until you know better. Then when you know better, do better."

WHEN YOU KNOW BETTER, DO BETTER

Twelve years later at thirty-seven years old going through a business break-up (granted, it was a different kind of break-up, but a break-up nonetheless), I followed Maya Angelou's advice. I knew better, so I did better…and I did so faster. My mindset toolbox was much heavier now. I spent a dozen years filling it up with new ways of thinking and taking note of those who faced unworthiness before me.

When the self-limiting belief visited me at a more mature age, the process of radical self-awareness and planning took weeks, not months or years. My point is that deconstructing your self-limiting beliefs is going to take time. One of the most critical things to do as you embark on this journey is to give yourself grace. I can honestly say that it took me close to forty years to understand how to do this.

The process of writing this book has been the epitome of the self-limiting belief journey. Over the course of the past seven months, I've had moments of self-doubt and uncertainty questioning why I am writing this book. Am I worthy of authorship? What if I don't achieve the sales I want? What if I don't impact people the way I want to? What difference does it make if my story isn't told? There's a litany of questions that have riddled my mind. Ever heard of imposter syndrome? This is when you experience a pattern of doubting your own skills, talents, or accomplishments. That is what I've felt at various points during the writing process.

It's the process my writing coach, Ashley Mansour, has developed that has made all the difference. At the beginning of the *Ignite Your Inner Author* writing program I joined, mindset was a vital module. Ashley prepared us for the limited thinking that would emerge based on demons that haunt us from our past. Through the practice of new habits, the strength of community support, and the magic of mentorship, our emerging author group was reminded that each of us are better than our excuses. In a Facebook Live she did, Ashley talked about courage—trusting ourselves, believing our unique message is worth sharing regardless of if the topic has been discussed before, moving beyond overwhelm and perfectionism, and not worrying about what comes next. The commitment to daily action, resilience through the valleys of uncertainty, and putting the readers first are what has taken me and many other new authors across the finish line.

In an interesting dichotomy, while actions become swifter and more confident when you master resilience, the process of self-discovery and healing is ever evolving. Healing can feel cyclical and even never-ending. It's because new wounds trigger old stories. We remember how we got the scars we still live with today. On the back of my left leg above my ankle, I have a small scar. The scar is from climbing a volcano while I was on a volunteer trip in Guatemala (you'll hear more about that trip in a later chapter). A piece of volcanic rock cut me and it was a small ordeal, but nothing I couldn't manage. Every time I see the scar, it reminds me of the climb, the chaos of the injury, and naturally everything that happened on that trip (thankfully most of it was positive). Just like physical scars, we have emotional scars. Wounds take time to heal and the scars they leave behind don't let us forget the pain we went through.

For example, if you experienced abuse of any kind at a young age and then went through a similar experience in your adulthood, the old memories of abuse may come flooding back to you. You might think of a past abuser and how they made you feel. How you dealt with your past experience will determine how you deal with a familiar experience today. Triggers can emerge at any time—just like hearing an old song on the radio. How many times have you heard a song that took you on a blast to the past? While we can admire, appreciate, or agonize over the past, the fact is, it's gone. The beautiful part of healing is when you can embrace the present and become curious about the future.

The example that hits home for me most closely is heartbreak. I'm challenged to trust because I have never experienced a relationship that abided by the established and agreed upon rules of fidelity and faithfulness. It's one of the reasons I chose to live a non-monogamous lifestyle. There's much more to that, but that is for a different book, so you'll have to stay tuned. Experiencing heartbreak more than once did not stop me from pursuing love again. I've chosen to be better, not bitter, and that entails choosing different strategies to achieve better results. The punchline here is that "doing better" for yourself is perpetual. Don't think about doing better as a destination. Consider it a journey. Now let's get into how to execute the five steps of A5 (Assess, Analyze, Adjust, Act, Align).

5

TO ASSESS IS THE BEGINNING OF SUCCESS

ANY TIME THERE IS AN icebreaker, and someone asks the question, "If you could be any animal, what would you be and why?" my answer is a bird, specifically a hawk. A hawk has a fifty-thousand-foot view of the world. When you consider the first A in A5, I want you to envision yourself as a hawk. The intent is for you to get up above your circumstance so you can honestly and accurately assess it. If you are amid what feels like a crisis now as you're reading this book, getting up above your circumstance may feel impossible. That's because you are in the early stages of grief. That's okay. Remember that it's okay to not be okay. You are more like an injured hawk, which means you may have to spend some time asking for help and guidance from others who have valuable perspective and expertise. Let those people lift you up so that you can see your circumstance more clearly. This may be a time you have to swallow your pride and step into vulnerability.

If vulnerability feels foreign to you, I encourage you to check out Brené Brown's book, *Daring Greatly: How the Courage to Be Vulnerable Transforms the Way We Live, Love, Parent, and Lead.* She helps readers recognize that vulnerability is where feelings like uncertainty, fear, and grief can co-exist with emotions like love, joy, and empathy. My favorite part of the book is when she says, "I want to be in the arena. I want to be brave with my life. And when we make the choice to dare greatly, we sign up to get our asses kicked. We can choose courage, or we can choose comfort, but we can't have both. Not at the same time. Vulnerability is not winning or losing; it's having the courage to show up and be seen when we have no control of the outcome. Vulnerability is not a weakness; it's our greatest measure of courage. A lot of cheap seats in the arena are filled with people who never venture onto the floor." Choose to be on the arena floor. Being vulnerable is required to do an honest self-assessment.

COLLECTING OBSERVATIONS

When assessing your self-limiting belief, it is important to review the full landscape of your life so you do not have blind spots. Blind spots are important not to miss because if you do, you may end up repeating the same mistakes. The purpose of an assessment is to determine themes. I have spent almost two decades in the consulting world, and a huge part of consulting methodology is assessment. It usually entails doing interviews and observations to gather as many vantage points as possible. This helps to draw accurate conclusions and recommendations. A self-assessment starts with asking yourself the important questions first, then getting insights from others. It is helpful to expand your perspective by asking others what their observations are and being open enough to receive their feedback. Outside perspective is an excellent way to learn more about your blind spots. My mom and sister would often tell me, for example, that people take my kindness as a weakness. They observed that I would get taken advantage of for being too kind and accommodating. I assumed (wrongly on occasion as my family would point out) that all people had good intentions. Assessment is also a process of acceptance. When you can accept the present, you create the capacity to expend energy on future steps instead of exerting all your energy on resisting reality (otherwise known as the denial phase of Kübler-Ross's cycle of grief as covered previously).

When I went through divorce, I did an in-depth assessment of myself—and an extended one. It took a long time for me to fly at fifty thousand feet. I suffered with unworthiness, so my initial assessment was on the wrong things. I was focused on the actions of my ex-husband and the emotions I was caught up in instead of examining my attitude and my actions. I was having a big fat pity party that was getting me nowhere except for having puffy eyes, which meant I could not even see the bottom of the ice cream pints in which I was indulging. One of the most critical things to remember in the assessment step is to scrutinize the only thing that you have control over and can change: yourself. It does not mean dismissing everything else. It means spending *most* of your time evaluating yourself. Can you think back to a time when you were resentful and incessantly thought about all the ways and all the reasons another person(s) was wrong? You blamed them for the situation you were in that felt like chaos and kept you on an emotional rollercoaster. What results did you yield by spending that time in agony, anger, despair, resentment, and/or rage? I have been there, sadly more times than I'd like to admit. That's how I know when you focus on others who have hurt or wronged you, you don't get far. You can't control or change others or a negative situation that has happened, but you can control your outlook, your attitude, and your future actions.

TAKING RESPONSIBILITY

Maturation of the self-assessment process is when you take personal responsibility and ownership for the things that are not working in your life. Pointing fingers and finding blame in others will keep you paralyzed. My epiphany in maturing through the assessment step included three realizations: 1) as mentioned earlier, I am the common denominator in each instance of limiting beliefs I encounter, and therefore I am best positioned to figure out how to grow from the circumstance, 2) ego needs to be set aside when developing the self, and 3) life is 10 percent what happens to you and 90 percent how you react. Ego and attitude are demons that we all battle with daily. The moment we stop fighting to be right and choose positivity and perseverance is when growth happens.

What observations did I make about the core elements (purpose, mindset, habits, inputs, and influences) when I pulled out my personal compass? This was an interesting exercise. Starting with purpose, my first observation was that I lost sight of my purpose in marriage. I was focused on more of my professional purpose than my personal purpose, which is a difficult balance to strike. I spent so much energy on being the best at work, getting promoted, and serving my clients to make healthcare better, but not much time on making my personal partnership better. I was self-absorbed and disconnected in my marriage—not all the time, but a lot of the time. When I took the emotion out of the situation (which took months to do), I realized it was not that I was unworthy of a long-term relationship, but one of the roadblocks to making my relationship successful was not investing in creating a partnership where we both contributed equally or collaborated on our goals. I signed up for marriage but lived like a person who was single and independent. I poured money into the marriage, but that was not a substitute for time and connection. Part of my assessment was also that before I started my career, I devoted a lot of energy to my relationship. When I became a healthcare professional, I did not dedicate time to fostering a stable ecosystem for my relationship to thrive.

The beginning of a relationship is like getting a new car. There's a rush that comes with a new car when you admire all its parts and features. You treat it delicately with care and make sure it's clean and ready to make an appearance. Over time if you don't maintain it—car washes, oil changes, yearly tune-ups, and so on—it won't function the same. It takes continuous commitment to keep a car running well. That's true for relationships too. After you put in all the work to find and build a commitment with a partner, the relationship must be continuously nurtured if it's going to retain its vibrancy.

What did I assess about my mindset in marriage? My mindset about marriage was that if I gave it money and sex, it would be successful. That was the wrong mindset. Money is great and so is sex. However, without consistent communication, emotional connection, shared goals, spontaneity, and ongoing playfulness, it was like baking a cake and forgetting the flour and sugar—there would be no structure or sweetness. This assessment sure was telling.

One of the reasons we shy away from this depth of personal assessment is because we do not like the answers we get. Assessing is recognizing what is not serving you, especially patterns, and taking responsibility and ownership over how you have contributed to a situation. In this case, my recognition was what I was *not* contributing to my marriage. Selfishness, neglect, and imbalance were themes that I needed to acknowledge and determine how to address so the same themes wouldn't emerge in the future. As evidenced by the stories I have shared, it is in the pain and struggle that we experience the most growth.

How was I doing on my habits? This element was not that hard to assess. I had one consistent habit: work. Looking back, that's an awful observation, certainly a key learning that I needed to take note of. I spent Monday through Thursday out of town with my clients and colleagues. When I was home Friday through Sunday, I prioritized work. The time I spent with my ex was at dinner, and sometimes if we had something planned with friends or family, we would do that together. The justification of my habits at the time was that if I put my devotion to work, it would give me more time later to spend on other things and with the people I cared about. The problem with creating habits like that is you are living for tomorrow and not for today. You miss out on so much of life this way. When you do an assessment of your habits, it is worthwhile to evaluate your tendencies. For example, my tendency has always been to gravitate toward school or work when other parts of life got hard. It is a form of avoidance, which is an unhealthy and subconscious habit. If I wanted more meaningful relationships, I could not spend forever avoiding the parts which require the most effort.

My inputs were no surprise, and not balanced either. My mind-body-spirit rating could be described as okay-bad-worst. Intellectually, I was in a decent place because I was constantly learning about business, consulting, and healthcare. I ate well and exercised sometimes, but my sleep pattern was not consistent. I did not spend time feeding my spirit. Overall, I was tired, but making good money, so I figured that was good enough. It wasn't too long into my career that I realized that money and happiness were not necessarily synonymous.

My influences were colleagues and books, my ex, and a small group of friends and family. This was the most vibrant part of my assessment because it was my influences that helped me to determine what direction I should go in my life during this trying season. Truthfully, it was my support system that kept me alive. When the consequences of divorce sunk in, I fell into a deep, dark, and dangerous depression. It got so bad that I contemplated suicide. I thought of everything from poisoning myself, drowning myself, cutting myself, hanging myself, and even jumping off a tall structure or bridge. My suicidal thoughts were driven by the desire to escape. I was ashamed of my short-lived marriage and didn't want to live in shame and guilt. I didn't want to explain myself to anyone. I didn't want to fathom starting over. I didn't want to face the questions that were coming my way. I didn't want to hear the judgments, opinions, or sometimes even advice from others. Suicide was simply an escape route. That may sound completely crazy to you. If you have never been depressed, then you may have a tough time processing the lengths our minds tell us to go.

Thanks to a healthy support system, I am living to write this book today. I am grateful that in my darkness, there were loving, supportive souls who could shine light into my life. The road was long and arduous to get out of my cave of sorrow. As a side note, if you or someone you know is suffering with suicidal thoughts, please call or text 988. It is a suicide and crisis lifeline. You can also visit: https://988lifeline.org. This resource was not available at the time I could have benefited from it. Don't be afraid to use it.

When you take responsibility for yourself and your actions, you are in an improved position to expand. Expansion is the opposite of limitation. One of the greatest ways to challenge your limits is to expand your viewpoint. It is like when you go to the eye doctor, and they change the lenses in front of your eyes, and you realize that there are some lenses that allow you to see much more clearly than others. The people you surround yourself with who are positive influences are like different pairs of glasses, which are necessary especially when the glasses you are wearing are foggy, blurry, or broken.

CHOOSING CHANGE

An example of someone who did a thorough assessment of his life was my podcast guest, relationship coach Robin Choe. I interviewed him in Episode 5 where he talked about hope and happiness after heartbreak. On the show, Robin discussed working through a limiting belief growing up that he was not desirable. He was also working on his ego. His self-assessment work became more urgent when Robin became a young father. He went through divorce, and for that period, he felt like his life turned upside down, but little did he know he would soon be helping countless men turn their lives right side up.

Just like my friend Kel Cal, Robin's message was in his mess. He did self-development work to be a better person and a better father. The overall assessment he made was around needing to show up differently for himself and his children. His assessment was so profound that he authored a book called *The HQ: How to Overcome Your Divorce and Be a Better Father*. The HQ stands for happiness quadrant. He breaks down the quadrants of health, wealth, relationships, and growth, giving dads practical tips for rebuilding and unlocking happiness after divorce. He turned his pain into power. Robin has built an inspiring community, and I admire how he was able to soar above his circumstance to assess, accept, and then grow from it. His assessment was undoubtedly a catalyst for his success.

Another great change example is from a popular Netflix series called *Sex/Life* that has ranked in trending and top shows in 2023. The assess step (also known as the first step) of the A5 (Assess, Analyze, Adjust, Act, Align) methodology was depicted in a compelling and vivid way in the show. The series is about a beautiful married mom of two named Billie who seems to have it all: a successful career, the perfect husband, two beautiful children, and a magnificent home on sprawling land in Greenwich, Connecticut. She had a life that many people aspire to live, only the ongoing challenge uncovered with each episode was this unrelenting feeling that she was not fully herself nor did she feel completely fulfilled. A run-in with her old flame, Brad reopened a sexual part of her that remained latent in her marriage. It ignited a deep exploration of herself and an assessment about what she truly wanted in her life. Her limiting belief was believing she had to live a life that was accepted by the masses even though she longed for something different.

Ultimately, Billie broke free from her limiting belief, and her honest self-assessment was that she wanted to end her nine-year marriage. She got feedback from her therapist and best friend to validate her observations, and then she made the decision that was best for her. Billie's assessment led to a series of choices that were judged by others but that she was at peace with because it meant choosing a path that was 100 percent authentic and true to who she was and how she wanted to live each day. Interestingly, her toughest critics, including her mother, ex, and friends, turned into people who grew to respect her for pursuing life on her own terms. Billie's self-acceptance, self-love, and self-assessment are what propelled her beyond the limited life she wanted desperately to get out of.

Like Rob and Billie—two divorced and driven individuals, I chose change. Choosing change is not easy. Whether change is positive or negative, it is disruptive. It is like switching from autopilot to manual navigation. The definition of insanity has been described as doing the same thing repeatedly and expecting different results. When you intentionally choose change, you are giving yourself a chance to achieve different results, pursue the fulfillment you desire, and live a life on your own terms. The stages of grief are real and inevitable, but the good news is that for every tumble down, there is a way back up.

Now grab a journal or notebook and a pen or find a place you like to write electronically, such as an iPad, tablet, or smartphone, because you'll be using it throughout the remainder of the book. You can label a section in your notes called A5 (Assess, Analyze, Adjust, Act, Align) Reflection. At the end of each chapter that describes the five steps of

A5, I'll provide you with a short set of questions to reflect on. Take a few minutes to answer each question.

WRITING AND REFLECTION PROMPT: ASSESSMENT QUESTIONS

1. *What self-limiting belief am I facing?*
2. *What is the source of my self-limiting belief?*
3. *What stage of grief am I experiencing? (See Kübler-Ross visual on page 64)*
4. *Who can give me feedback and bring awareness to any blind spots I may have?*

6

ANALYZE TO RISE

SHAKIRA'S HIPS DON'T LIE. NEITHER does data. I am a true crime junkie. I watch everything from *Dateline* and *20/20* to *Law and Order: SVU* and true crime documentaries on Netflix. When a crime happens, data is collected in a few different ways so that the crime can be solved. Fingerprints, bodily fluid, hair follicles, shoe prints, cell phone records, cell tower pings, video camera surveillance, credit card transactions, text messages, email messages, direct messages (DMs), social media posts, and receipts are all examples of data points that help investigators solve a crime. I want you to go from flying high in the sky like a hawk to a crime scene investigator with a magnifying glass. Now, imagine putting that magnifying glass on your self-limiting belief and surrounding circumstances that drive the story behind why you think that belief is true.

BECOMING A CRIME SCENE INVESTIGATOR

What information had I collected at the crime scenes throughout my life that told me the story "I am unworthy"? The analyze step is about synthesizing the data you have collected. Here are snippets that play in short clips across my mind like a series of stories on Instagram:

I am unworthy of help because independence means doing things on my own.

I am unworthy of wealth because my parents were not wealthy.

I am unworthy of love because I have been divorced.

I am unworthy of being at the top because I do not match the profile of those who are there.

I am unworthy of being fully respected because I did not accomplish motherhood.

I am unworthy of inclusion because I do not believe in monogamy.

I am unworthy of success as a podcaster because there are no examples who look like me.

The crazy thing about these data points is that they are based in *fear*—false evidence appearing real. I point this out because we can sometimes mistake fears as universal truths. Fears are merely our own truths. Our fears may not be true to the outsider looking in. When searching for evidence to support these claims, I am hard-pressed. A limiting belief is like an illusion—things that we see, or think are there but are not real or are distorted. Our minds can imprison us with false truths if we are not careful. The most valuable thing I have learned about fear is from American World War II veteran George Addair who said, "Everything you've ever wanted is sitting on the other side of fear" (also reiterated by renowned American author, Jack Canfield). Analysis is the catalyst to rising above fear.

The real data comes from understanding the origin of our self-limiting beliefs. All the thoughts I share above are the truths I once believed. To unpack each of these, I needed to find the root cause. I will pick out one that every now and then still pops up and pesters me: "I am unworthy of being fully respected because I did not accomplish motherhood." What was the root of this limited thinking? This claim made its debut after I got married (probably more like when I got engaged). As many moms are with the best of intentions, my mom was eager for me to have a baby. So were other people; it felt like everyone. I was asked by my family, friends, and perfect strangers (I still am today) when I would be having a baby. Motherhood was and is seen as an achievement. It is common to hear someone say that being a mom is the hardest job there is and how stay-at-home moms have it harder than anyone. There is even a day every year that celebrates moms.

In my twenties I was told that I was lucky to be young because it meant I had time to become a mom. Then in my thirties I was told that it still was not too late, and I got the bonus commentary around how I could freeze my eggs to ensure I could have kids later in life. It is funny how I cannot remember a single person asking me if I even wanted kids. If asked, I would have responded with "no" and hoped I would be respected for it. I hear people say that being a mom is the best thing that has ever happened to them. I get questioned to this day around why I do not want to have children as if it were some kind of illness I should be hospitalized for. It is merely a preference. I love kids; I simply do not desire to have my own at this time. It's not to say that can't ever change, but that's what I feel at this stage of my life. I have been questioned so much that it makes me feel less than. It is a crappy feeling. The origin of this limiting belief was not living up to the expectations of others.

To combat the limiting thought that not being a mom made me less than, I needed new data so I could tell a new story. I looked for examples of well-respected, successful, and influential women who did not have children—Oprah Winfrey, Ellen DeGeneres, Tracee Ellis Ross, Jennifer

Aniston, Elizabeth Dole, and Condoleezza Rice to name a few. I think these women have done decent for themselves; therefore, I have confidence that I will do just fine…heck maybe even better than fine. Furthermore, in the twenty-first century, there are far more diverse ways that people live. Non-conventional relationships, partnerships, and parenting scenarios are pervasive. Women are choosing not to have children for a variety of reasons such as the desire to live a more flexible life or to be free from a huge financial responsibility. There is nothing wrong with choosing to live a non-traditional life. In moments when I feel like I am not living up to someone else's expectations of me, it is when I harness my message, "Be unapologetically you." I am fabulous just the way I am. I take care of my stuffed animal unicorns and dog brothers as if they were humans. That must count for something!

On the flipside, what about the narrative that women tell themselves because of becoming a mother? There's a whole set of limiting beliefs I have heard from women who do have kids.

I can no longer be sexy or desirable.

I won't be able to pursue my dreams with kids.

The dreams of my kids are more important than mine.

I can't climb a career ladder and be a good mom.

The fun part of my life is over.

Having kids doesn't mean you and your dreams must become smaller. It just means that the way you prioritize your time changes. I have seen the most tremendous moms accomplish everything they want in life.

My good friend Kandi raised three incredible sons with her husband, and after they were independent enough, she went back to school to get her PhD and is now a faculty member at a prestigious university and has become an author. While she raised her kids, she had a very successful consulting career and found the time that was right for her to pivot to her academic pursuits.

My best friend Katie is raising two sons and a niece with her husband and during the pandemic pursued her dream to become a labor and delivery nurse. She went to nursing school, graduated with astounding grades, and today, she does what she loves while also being a mom.

My friend Mafae Yunon-Belasco is one of the most impressive female entrepreneurs and moms that I know. She is the mega mom of six marvelous children and has years of dominating and achieving prominent success in the beauty and pageant industry, including landing top five in the Miss World competition 2003. She's the founder of Mafae Management Consultancy and co-owner with her husband of a sports academy, the Belasco Unlimited Skills Academy. She's a business leader in the Philippines, Australia, and the United States. She built her success brick by brick.

You see, there is no linear path. There's only your path, and that's going to look different than everyone else's path. When you focus on what you want for you, what the rest of the world is doing around you doesn't really have a major impact on you (unless you let it).

I'll delve into one more narrative: "I am unworthy of inclusion because I do not believe in monogamy." Where does this self-limiting belief come from? This is a fun one to break down. I grew up in the Catholic faith with conservative beliefs. Be with one person at a time, get married, procreate, believe in God, pray in times of doubt, be obedient to hierarchy—these are the things I was taught. Today, I am not with one person at a time, am no stranger to divorce, don't have children, believe in universal energy, turn to humans before God in doubtful moments, and don't subscribe to much hierarchical structure in my life. In other words, I am living life the exact opposite of what I was taught. I don't say that to sound rebellious, but these are the data points that are real.

Based on the political landscape we are in, the world is dominantly a Christian conservative one. The acceptance of same-sex marriage is not as widespread as it could be, racism is alive and well, Donald Trump wants to run for president of the United States of America again, and *Roe v. Wade* was overturned. I cringe writing these facts, but they are indeed facts. This landscape doesn't exactly promote a warm and cozy space of psychological safety for me. I don't align with what much of the world believes. Make no mistake: do not read what I share about my own beliefs to mean that I expect others to believe as I do. I want to live in a world where we can embrace our differences peacefully and respectfully. I do hope to see positive progress toward more unification in my lifetime. I remain cautiously optimistic.

The question is then begged, how do I break through this limitation? The answer is that I am doing it every day in how I choose to show up in the world. In politics, we hear that change starts at the kitchen table. Well, let's just say that over the past few years, I have sat down at a lot of tables and explained my lifestyle to a variety of people—mostly close people in my life, my mom, sister, best friends, and even some colleagues and other associates. I've been comforted surprisingly in that every person I love and care about has accepted me for me. That's been a huge aspect of breaking through this limitation. The best way I have found to thrive is in community. I have built an incredible community of like-minded people, and now part of my coaching is dedicated to people who want to explore their own curiosities about non-monogamy.

THE FIFTH AGREEMENT

When limited thinking begins to influence you, the analyze step is meant to have you do a gut check on your purpose, mindset, habits, inputs, and influences. Analysis helps you determine if where you are is where you want to be, or if you want to experience something else. An author I admire is Don Miguel Ruiz. One of the books he wrote was *The Fifth Agreement*. It is the update and sequel to the wildly popular book *The Four Agreements*, one of my all-time favorite books. The fifth agreement is to be skeptical but learn to listen. It is further described as, "Don't believe yourself or anybody else unconditionally. Use the power of doubt to question everything you hear: is it really the truth? Listen to the intent behind the words and you will understand the real message." In other words, part of growth is to question things, including yourself because we evolve every day.

I've applied the fifth agreement to a limiting belief that I still battle with, which is that racism feels impossible to improve in America because there are countless facts illustrating our regression despite historic progress like the Civil Rights movement. Senseless deaths like Eric Garner, Philando Castile, Breonna Taylor, George Floyd, and many others have reinforced this conclusion. I am skeptical about the advancement of diversity, equity, inclusion, and belonging (DEI&B) in America, but I have learned to listen to what's changing and advancing like having the first female minority, Kamala Harris, as vice president of the United States.

In my consulting work, I am helping healthcare organizations to advance their DEI&B agendas. While I question the speed of meaningful change, I am inspired by the trailblazers who came before me like Martin Luther King Jr., Harriet Tubman, and Malcom X. I also know that I can and have made a difference by being an ally to the disenfranchised, maintaining a podcast platform where voices can be heard, and being the change that I want to see in the world. The fifth agreement is about not just accepting what is but staying in pursuit of what you want things to be. What are the things that you are questioning, and what analysis are you making to impact those things for the better?

THE ANALYZE EXERCISE

Pull out the personal life compass. Consider the ratings and reflection questions below.

	Rate each on a scale of 1 to 5 1 = doing poorly 5 = doing excellent	Reflection Questions
Purpose		What am I doing to align to my purpose?
Mindset		What is my current mindset manifesting?
Habits		What habits are/are not serving me?

	Rate each on a scale of 1 to 5 1 = doing poorly 5 = doing excellent	Reflection Questions
Inputs		What inputs should I continue/change?
Influences		What influences would I benefit most from?

As you consider your answers and reflections, notice where you may need to spend more time. Using the business break-up example and walking myself through the analyze step was extremely valuable. Here is how I filled out the table.

	Rate each on a scale of 1 to 5 1 = doing poorly 5 = doing excellent	Reflection Answers
Purpose	4	I am reaching people through podcasting. I need to create a new platform to continue my mission driven work.

	Rate each on a scale of 1 to 5 1 = doing poorly 5 = doing excellent	Reflection Answers
Mindset	3	I am manifesting a magnificent new partnership. **I am working on the limiting belief that I may not achieve long-term success with my brand and podcast.**
Habits	2	**My sleep pattern is not serving me. My daily routine could benefit from more consistent weekly time to strategize.**
Inputs	4	My exercise is consistent. I could cut down on cheat foods. Podcasts and audiobooks continue to be great motivation.
Influences	5	My community and five people I spend the most time with have helped me stay strong through this transitional period.

This is a high-level analysis. You could go even further and do daily or monthly tracking. Even a brief analysis provides insights on what requires more attention in your life. Based on the analysis I did, it was evident that the areas of my life that needed more attention were mindset and habits. If I expected to be successful with Born Unbreakable and everything associated with it, I needed to shift my mindset and improve my daily routine.

One of the guests I was deeply inspired by was Rosa Alanis. Rosa is the founder of Pro Lifts. In Episode 3, she tells her story about persevering through the pandemic. A self-limiting belief she battled with was that she was not smart enough. The pandemic challenged her will, and she proved to herself that she was not only smart enough, but also capable of thriving. The analyze step played a significant role in her ability to overcome her self-limiting belief. The pandemic took a huge toll on Rosa's fitness business. Prior to the pandemic, Rosa signed a contract for a new fitness space to rent out. COVID-19 brought in-person interactions to a halt at the start of 2020. Rosa's business model was built entirely on doing one-on-one and group fitness coaching in person. She had the major fiscal responsibility of paying rent on her new space. She went through all the A5 steps. The analyze step helped her devise her adjustments, actions, and alignment. Rosa's conviction to help people achieve their best health did not waver. Through research and creativity, data proved she could pursue a virtual model of fitness coaching. Analyzing is about having a solution-oriented mindset. You do not dwell on the problem; you open your mind to innovative solutions. Rosa's deep commitment to her why, her positive mindset, her healthy inputs, and her influence of faith are what carried her through analyzing and pivoting to keep her business from closing.

FORMAL SELF-ASSESSMENTS

The analyze step is eye-opening because its emphasis is on facts over feelings. In the assess stage, like the early stages of the five stages of grief, you can feel highly emotional because you may be freshly uncovering new revelations about yourself. When you begin to accept your assessment, then you can shift into fact finding. I have collected data quite a bit through the years via well-known self-assessments such as (note that you can Google any of these to learn more and obtain access):

1. The DiSC® Assessment (paid)—examines how an individual ranks in four primary personality types: dominance, influence, steadiness, and conscientiousness.
2. Strengths Finder (paid)—measures thirty-four research-validated talents; themes then guide the development of those talents into strengths to succeed at work and in life.

3. Attachment Style Quiz (free)—explores how child-hood conditioning manifests into your adult relationships in these four styles: anxious, avoidant, disorganized, or secure.

4. Love Languages Test (free)—examines how an individual prefers to receive love: through words of affirmation, physical touch, quality time, gifts, or acts of service.

5. 16Personalities Test (free)—determines the dominant personality type amongst sixteen types highlighting what drives, inspires, and worries each.

6. Management by Strengths (paid)—assesses temperament, communication style, what motivates individuals, and how each temperament reacts in work and social settings.

7. Hogan Assessment (paid)—measures everyday strengths, how strengths manifest in times of stress, and values to predict future workplace performance.

Personality tests (several are free as you can see) like these highlight your tendencies, strengths, and pitfalls. These insights are a good indicator of how you might struggle with self-limiting beliefs. For example, my tendencies are people pleasing and conflict avoidance; therefore, caring about and managing other people's opinions has historically been challenging for me. Knowing my challenge areas has helped me work on setting boundaries and conflict management. Conversely, your strengths can help you get to the other side of your limitations.

Check out https://www.16personalities.com/free-personality-test as a free place to start if you are new to these kinds of assessments. The free tests are a great way to understand yourself in the context of personal relationships and dominant characteristics. For example, if you are struggling with a self-limiting belief around unworthiness in love and intimate relationships, the Attachment Style or Love Language quiz may help analyze what your tendencies are and how you can shift your mindset to get closer to what you are seeking in a healthy intimate relationship. An avoidant type of attachment style may need to work on more intentional communication, and a person who receives love through words of affirmation may need to get exposure to the other love languages to better connect with how a partner best receives love. If we don't have the analytical data to expose how we are wired and show up in the world which form the perceptions of the people around us, we will be hard-pressed to make meaningful changes to better manage ourselves and strengthen areas we've formerly been challenged by.

The paid assessments are often great for business settings as they raise your awareness around who you are as a colleague and leader. The first paid assessment I would recommend is the Strengths Finder because you can obtain it via a book called *Now, Discover Your Strengths* by Marcus

Buckingham and Donald O. Clifton, PhD. You can purchase a book for as little as ten dollars, and you get access to the online assessment. The book shows you how to develop your unique talents and strengths, which is valuable for both life and business. You may have a limiting belief, for example, around not being smart enough in business. If you discover your strengths, you'll be better positioned to leverage them to your advantage and identify those around you who complement those strengths to create exponential momentum with your business endeavors. Your confidence can grow with the right mindset, and you can begin to break down any self-limiting belief that has held you back from living the life you truly desire.

WRITING AND REFLECTION PROMPT: ANALYZE QUESTIONS

1. *What evidence is there to support the self-limiting belief I am having?*
2. *What do I need to spend time focusing on to shift my thinking? (See personal compass on page 60)*
3. *What support (e.g., from others or resources) do I need right now?*

7

ADJUST TWO-MILLIMETER SHIFTS AT A TIME

I MOVED TO LAS VEGAS, Nevada, from Brentwood, in Northern California, in the summer of 2021. Assessing and analyzing helped me to make this major life change. Earlier that year in the spring, I found myself evaluating my expensive California lifestyle. California likes to impose heavy taxes—even more when you file your taxes solo with no children. Maybe I should have listened to all the people who kept nagging me about having children...kidding. My mom, who lived with me, was also contemplating if this was the year she would retire. If she retired, I thought to myself, "What would she do for fun as a retiree living in the suburbs?" We lived near wineries, but she did not drink wine or any alcohol for that matter. She could spend more time with her granddaughters (my sister's kids), but they were getting older, and surely their time would be filled with more teenage activities. We had family in Las Vegas, it wasn't too far, and Nevada didn't have income tax. The data pointed us to Sin City, and off we went.

TRANSITIONING

Think back to a time when you went through a life transition—a relationship status change, a move, a career shift, starting a family. Something happens when you make transitions in life: adjustments. The internationally acclaimed business strategist and author, Tony Robbins, often talks about two-millimeter shifts. His message is about how the next level of your achievements is not that far away. It is just two millimeters to go from where you are to the next outstanding level. Change does not have to be drastic. It can happen little by little. When I moved to a new state, it hit me that just about everything in my life was going to change—who I spent my time with, what activities I would do, places I would visit, and my overall routine. Thanks to technology I could stay in touch every day with my sister and friends in California. It was difficult to adjust to new surroundings at first. I danced with that same self-limiting belief of unworthiness as I reflected on my ability to successfully start over.

It was time to pull out my personal compass again. I assessed my life and analyzed the data to get to a new place that would lead me to a new level, and I needed to continue with adjusting. I spent four months at this point leaning into my new brand, Born Unbreakable. My purpose to help people crush their self-limiting beliefs was alive and well. I expanded my mindset to think of more ways to reach and influence people, and I was figuring out what adjustments could be valuable to make in my inputs and influences.

If I wanted to reach more people, I would need to connect with more podcast guests, produce more content, and release more episodes. I increased my networking presence in podcasting communities and the number of episodes I recorded. Instead of releasing four episodes per month, I would release eight.

My health and wellness needed adjustment too. In California, I had a diet and exercise routine that was consistent, and it was thrown way out of whack after moving. I let go of the reins on my diet. I was eating unhealthy foods several times a day on some days (darn the twenty-four-seven Vegas nightlife!)—we're talking pizza, nachos, ice cream, and all the other goodies that remind me of what the "freshman fifteen" meant back in college. Bad eating habits impacted my energy and drive. My exercise regimen was nonexistent some weeks, which was completely out of character for me. I reminisced on how I *used to* be able to do challenging obstacle courses and long-distance runs and couldn't fathom what those felt like anymore. When my clothes got tighter and my energy got lower, enough was enough.

I slowly started making changes by eating healthier and going to my community gym more frequently. Then I got a membership at the larger athletic club to have access to personal training and a variety of fitness classes. On my fortieth birthday weekend in January of 2023, I decided to stop drinking alcohol. Not only did I feel like I had my fair share of libations through the past two decades, but the reflection of my father dying at forty years old nudged me too. He was a brilliant man who made terrible health choices, and I didn't want to perpetuate them.

In spring of 2023, I decided to join a six-week transformation program at a local kickboxing studio. This meant eating healthy foods every day (no cheat days or splurges), kickboxing a minimum of three days per week, taking supplements, and tracking my progress via weekly pictures and weight and measurement checks. I met my goal to lose twenty pounds, and the following month, I participated in a second fitness challenge and lost an additional five pounds (that's a total of twenty-five pounds in less than ninety days). I didn't drink any sodas during the fitness programs and didn't miss it afterwards. I have kept soda out of my diet permanently. A healthy lifestyle wasn't new to me. I just strayed away from it a little bit too far and needed to find my way back to better habits. The adjustment put me back on track to a sustainable healthy lifestyle.

I also needed to expand my influences because I wanted to grow my Vegas network. This required me to put myself out there by socializing more and taking initiative to make meaningful connections. My awesome real estate agent Sebastian and dedicated loan officer Maxine have become dear friends who have continued to introduce me to great people. My friend Noah, who is a sensationally successful entertainment entrepreneur too, has introduced me to other influential go-getters. The kickboxing studio and Aaron's entertainment and corporate networks have been sources for new friendships too. I've spent more time with family and friends who at one point also had to adjust to Vegas as a new living location. It was daunting at first, but with each month that has gone by, progress has been positive. Incrementally, my network has grown, and as a result, my entrepreneurial spirit and outlook has too.

I have been in Las Vegas for over two years, and the two-millimeter shifts are still occurring. As entrepreneur and philanthropist Marie Forleo once said, "Success doesn't come from what you do occasionally; it comes from what you do consistently."

I facilitated a ninety-day program called Born a Boss Babe. During the program, guest experts joined us to discuss the topics of relationships, wealth, networking, goal setting, health and wellness, and continuous learning. For the continuous learning session, the objective was for participants to consider ways they could sustain new practices learned from the program, especially in areas they wanted to focus on. My guest expert and friend was DJ Cardenas (author, speaker, coach, and leadership expert). He had a message that was akin to two-millimeter shifts. It was to focus on 1 percent improvement each day. DJ's message was simple, effective, and doable. An improvement of 1 percent is a commitment to being better than the day before. It's establishing the consistency and discipline to persevere in the areas that matter most to you so you can elevate your habits, accelerate your goals, and overcome your self-limiting beliefs.

In adjustment is where tenacity and grit are built. When you overcome, make a shift, and can sustain a new habit long enough, it becomes a part of your central operating system. You become more confident in your abilities. You begin to focus on the outcomes you want and less on the details of how you'll achieve them. You reinforce a belief system within yourself of a "yes, I can" attitude. Every time you're faced with a new obstacle that tests your self-belief, you remember what it was like to adjust, overcome, and persevere. In times of self-doubt and self-sabotage, those memories of successful pivots will remind you of exactly what you're made of: MORE.

Based on my self-analysis shared in the previous chapter, I needed to invest more time debunking the idea that I wouldn't be successful at growing the Born Unbreakable brand. I realized that I was fear-based and focused on everything that could go wrong instead of everything that could go right. That's called survival mode. If I wanted to be in a thriver mode, I needed to adjust by shifting my attention to solutions and outcomes. I did this by getting excited about what was possible, applying the experience I learned from my previous podcast, harnessing the power of my why, and recalling that being a mission driven messenger requires the courage to do new things.

The other epiphany I had was that what once was new soon becomes familiar. Just look at the era of COVID-19. In March of 2020, did you honestly believe that you would live through several years of a global pandemic? I don't think many people had confidence that grim spring. Being stuck inside like some sort of twisted social experiment was not exactly the kind of 2020 vision the world was hoping for. Just like Rosa Alanis adjusted, the whole world did. We found new ways of doing business, communications, relationships, celebrations, and self-care. Zoom calls became a new norm. We will always face uncertainty. Approaching that uncertainty with a curious mind, an open heart, and enthusiasm for new adventures and learning makes taking action a lot more fun.

THE PROCESS OF PATIENCE

One of the points I want to emphasize about adjusting is the importance of patience. What is your relationship with patience? Are you patient with yourself? Are you patient with your progress? As we approach the height of the digital revolution, I have observed that patience has dwindled in the world. This is exacerbated by our highly virtual world which a global pandemic has normalized. Instacart, Amazon, and Uber bring goods and services to our doorstep—sometimes in only a few hours. When posts are released into the world of Instagram, Facebook, Twitter, Snapchat, TikTok, or YouTube, posters anxiously watch their likes, comments, shares, and perhaps even await that magic moment of going viral. This is the era of instant gratification.

I remember when I first watched *The Social Dilemma*. It is a documentary that was released on Netflix in 2020. It highlights how social media's design nurtures addiction to maximize profit and manipulate people's emotions and behaviors. Your social media feed is a thoughtfully curated reel of information and ads that tantalize your political palette, stimulate your retail rage, and fuel your digital dopamine. All this digitization impacts our relationship with patience.

My plea is to remind you that despite the speed of celebrity newsbreaks, that's not how progress in life works. Don't get caught up in the comparison game social media brings either. As former President Theodore Roosevelt once said, "Comparison is the thief of joy." Stay the course, practice patience, don't be distracted by the journey of other people, and celebrate your wins along the way. Adjusting and sustaining excellence at each level you reach takes consistent discipline.

One of the guests who has continued to impress me as I have followed his journey is Australian motivational speaker and coach Luke Chlebowicz, a.k.a. Luke Mindpower. He has mastered the two-millimeter shift. I met Luke at the end of 2019. We both joined Lewis Howes's Inner Circle where like-minded, motivated world changers network and collaborate. We both have been guests on each other's podcast shows. His show is called *The Luke Mind Power Podcast*. Luke spent years prior to diving deep into self-development imprisoned by his trauma, choosing mediocre relationships and suffering through drug addiction. In 2019, Luke was growing his inspirational brand and showing up on social media daily with inspirational posts and videos. He had north of five thousand followers on Instagram who were loyal, including myself. He is one of the most consistent influencers I have watched stay dedicated to growing his community of dream chasers.

When I interviewed Luke in the summer of 2021, he had over 151,000 followers on TikTok because he started incorporating dancing into his motivational videos, so he was an inspirational entertainer. A little over eighteen months later, Luke has 472,000 followers on Instagram, 1.1 million followers on TikTok, and 10.4 million likes (and counting). To grow his brand and his following, he has shown up every single day year after year. It was not overnight. That is what adjustment looks like. Doing the daily work, being innovative, and putting yourself out there is how you persevere.

TRACKING YOUR PROGRESS

Tracking is one of the best ways to monitor your adjustment progress. There is no one-size-fits-all method to do this, but here are ideas to consider. The discipline and consistency of tracking will help to normalize new behaviors.

Ideas to help you track your adjustment progress	
1	Journal (free writing) for ten to fifteen minutes per day.
2	Download a habit tracker app (e.g., Done, Productive, Strides).
3	Use a whiteboard or wall calendar to track your progress.
4	Track tally marks on post-it notes in a place you are in daily.
5	Review your tracking progress with an accountability partner.

New York Times number-one bestselling author James Clear talks in his book, *Atomic Habits*, about how on average, it takes sixty-six days (more than two months) to build a new behavior or habit. Understand that it takes time for two-millimeter shifts to become your standard practice. April Garcia, whom I mentioned before, facilitated the mastermind I was in. The principle of a mastermind is described by Napoleon Hill, author of *Think and Grow Rich*, in 1937 as, "The coordination of knowledge and effort between two or more people who work towards a definite purpose in a spirit of harmony…no two minds every come together without thereby creating a third, invisible tangible force, which may be likened to a third mind," also known as the mastermind. My mastermind was attended by me, Bethany, Chris, Erica, Lauren, and Nichole (a.k.a. my accountability group of likeminded people from all over the U.S. and Puerto Rico). There have been other members along the way and intersections with other mastermind groups too. We met weekly to discuss wins, progress, reflections, and work collectively on ongoing growth and goals. It's a sacred space to stay elevated and encouraged. One year, Chris and Nichole both committed to doing the "75 Hard Challenge" invented by entrepreneur and podcaster Andy Frisella. For seventy-five days, the rules of the challenge are:

1. **Follow a diet**. While it can be a diet of your choosing, the diet must be a structured eating plan with the goal of physical improvement. No alcohol or meals outside your chosen diet are allowed.
2. **Complete two forty-five-minute workouts**, one of which must be outdoors.
3. **Take a progress picture**.
4. **Drink one gallon of water**.
5. **Read ten pages of a book** (audiobooks not included).

No alterations can be made to the program, and if any part of the daily goals is not completed, your progress resets to day one.

Each day that Chris and Nichole completed the challenge, they would mark off a day in their tracking system so they could see their progress—how far they went and how much further they had to go. There were times when they had to start over, and yes, that was painful for them. We still celebrated their two-millimeter shifts because despite their errors, both committed to sticking to it and starting over. Notice how the challenge is longer than two months. For some people, it may be that they stick to the routine even after seventy-five days are reached. The purpose of the program is transformative mental toughness, although a byproduct certainly is physical fitness improvement.

Another example of tracking success is from one of my podcast guests. In Episode 131 of my podcast show, I interviewed real estate investor and author Ralph DiBugnara. He is someone who knows very well the value of incremental progress and measuring for success. At a young age, Ralph mixed himself up with the wrong crowd who were getting into trouble and on the criminal fast track. He failed at school, so he felt like an outcast. Ralph was fortunate to be offered the opportunity to get into the mortgage and real estate industry and never looked back.

Ralph bought his first property when he was twenty-three years old and built a healthy portfolio. When the

2008 housing market crashed, Ralph lost everything. The self-limiting belief he had to overcome was not feeling like he was good enough or belonged. At low points like the market crash, it took Ralph tremendous focus and determination to persevere. The good news for Ralph is that he had evidence that in the years prior to 2008, he gradually made two-millimeter shifts to acquire real estate success, so undoubtedly, he had the skills to do it again. In all his businesses (e.g., closing mortgage loans, managing long and short-term rentals, and running a podcast), he measures his sales and key performance indicators so he can collaborate with his teams on how to make improvements through market research, finding smart deals, enhanced training, recruitment, and networking, and innovation. Ralph's systems and processes were developed over time through trial, error, and experience. His wealth and success grew through discipline and consistency two-millimeter shifts at a time. He mastered playing the long game. Ralph closed his episode with the final piece of advice to "bet on yourself more." When you trust in yourself and your abilities, you'll be amazed at what can happen.

Let's not forget about the tracking associated with my previously mentioned fitness journey. I used the My Accountability Plus app to upload weekly progress photos of my body from three different angles and photos of groceries I was buying and meals I was eating. I also entered weekly statistics (weight and body measurements). The act of tracking my two-millimeter shifts and being accountable to a group of fitness coaches was the cake topper to my transformational success. I doubt that without tracking I would have achieved my weight loss goal. In fact, I am confident that while I would have gotten close, the goal would not be met.

A book I highly recommend is *The Gap and The Gain: The High Achievers' Guide to Happiness, Confidence, and Success* by Dan Sullivan and Dr. Benjamin Hardy. If you have rumbled in the jungle with self-limiting beliefs, this book will help to shift your mindset. The message of the book is that unsuccessful people focus on "The Gap," and successful people focus on "The Gain." By acknowledging the two-millimeter shifts that you are making and celebrating your progress and wins, you will gain confidence and thrive in a gain mentality. If you stay stuck on what has not gone right, the obstacles you might face ahead, and letting perfect be the enemy of progress, you will fall victim to the gap mentality where you experience frustration, disappointment, and guilt. Enjoy and appreciate the process of adjusting. When you focus on the gain, your morale improves, you have an appreciation for the progress you've made, you acknowledge the people who have contributed to your journey, and you maintain an abundance mindset by recognizing what you have done vs. what you haven't.

WRITING AND REFLECTION PROMPT: ADJUST QUESTIONS

1. *What gains or wins can I celebrate?*
2. *What adjustments ("two-millimeter shifts") can I make today?*
3. *What results do I want to see in my life in the next six months?*

8

ACTION SEPARATES THE
BEST FROM THE REST

WHAT SEPARATES THE BEST FROM the rest is one simple word: ACTION. In a previous chapter, I talked about the process of analyzing. A note of caution is not to fall into the trap of analysis paralysis. Collect data. Weigh your options. Follow your gut. Then act. If you want to be a crusher of self-limiting beliefs, action is your best weapon. A dichotomy we face is that we want instant gratification and the convenience of tangible items at our fingertips, yet when it comes to the intangibles like making decisions that can change the trajectory of our lives, we ruminate incessantly. Why is that? It comes back around to the concept of internal versus external. When it comes to external things we want to acquire that create those quick dopamine hits of temporary satisfaction, time is of the essence. There is not much hesitation to act with external decisions. Internal purpose, mindset, and habits have long-term implications and could either result in positive outcomes or have dire consequences. The weight of responsibility is heavier, and the thought process is more complex, and that's why internal decisions are more difficult and take more time to make. To quench the quiet desperation felt inside and to answer the burning internal questions we face, action is the answer.

Did you know that action helps to produce happy chemicals from our brain? Those chemicals are dopamine, oxytocin, serotonin, and endorphins. Dopamine is a reward chemical that's produced when you do things like complete a task or celebrate a win. Oxytocin is the love hormone triggered by things like giving compliments or providing compassion. Serotonin is the mood stabilizer triggered by things like meditating or walking in nature. Endorphins are the pain killer produced by actions like laughter, eating chocolates, or watching a comedy.

So, one way to get excited about action is considering the happy chemicals you're helping to stir up inside of you. Of course, happiness is not a state we're supposed to remain in constantly, but when it comes to overcoming self-limiting beliefs, it sure helps to know how to produce more positivity. Dr. Loretta Breuning discusses how to retrain your brain to produce more of these happy chemicals in Episode 145 of my podcast show. One of the things

I appreciate that she discusses is how we're conditioned to act based on our upbringing and what we've experienced in our childhood.

To bring the concept of retraining your brain to life using endorphins as a happy chemical example, here are ways that you can make taking action more rewarding for yourself. Since taking action is not always easy, setting up a reward system can serve as a motivator. Writing this book is something that was challenging for me at times. How could I get motivated to sit down for several hours and write? Setting micro goals and rewarding myself for achieving them was one idea. For example, if my goal for a day was to write one thousand words, I'd choose a reward I could give myself once I reached one thousand words, like ordering the product I wanted from Amazon or going to get a cup of frozen yogurt. You might be ultra-excited to watch a new movie you've been anticipating for months. Use watching the movie as a reward for completing a task that you may have been procrastinating on (I'll be talking about procrastination in the next section).

A limiting belief several of my podcast guests struggled through was whether they were capable of being an entrepreneur because of the overwhelm associated with all the steps, such as creating a clear brand message, building a website, determining a marketing strategy, establishing a social media presence, generating leads, figuring out what systems to implement in their business, hiring and training the right team, and thriving in a competitive marketplace. In this example, one way to reduce the overwhelm is to focus on the parts instead of everything all at once. The reward system is helpful because it makes the process of launching a new business fun. You could set attainable daily actions, and for completing that day's set of actions, you could give yourself a reward (taking a bubble bath, eating your favorite meal, watching a few episodes of a show you love, or buying something that's been on your wish list). Consistent two-millimeter shifts coupled with a simple reward system is a powerful combination.

Going back to the early chapter where I highlight the origins of our self-limiting beliefs, there could be self-sabotaging behavior from our past that prevents us from taking healthy, happy, productive action. It may take deconditioning and reprogramming to develop habits that allow you to thrive in action (not staying stuck on thoughts of what did not work out in the past, trying new practices like meditation or walking, or talking to a mental health professional to heal from traumatic experiences). The stories in this chapter will provide you with insights on how people from all walks of life and experiences have taken successful action.

ACTION OVER EXCUSES

Action is one of the most consistent messages my podcasts guests discuss. I enjoyed the way the serial entrepreneur, business coach, and founder of 365 Driven, Tony Whatley, said it in Episode 127 of my podcast show: "Nowadays, I think people just get into this consumption pattern… and they never take action, so start today, take the first steps today." The context of his statement was around how people will keep going to conferences and listening to podcasts and books but are never ready to act. Tony is the epitome of action. One of his self-limiting beliefs was that if he made $100,000, he would be successful. In other words, he limited his earning potential. Through years of business experiences, he learned how outdated that thinking was. Tony was successful in the oil and gas industry, managing over $100 million of international projects, but knew that he was made for more. He decided to start LS1Tech, an online performance community for car lovers like him. Tony didn't overthink. He learned along the way, and after growing the community to several hundred thousand users, he sold the business for millions of dollars. He wrote the book *SideHustle Millionaire*, which I highly recommend reading or listening to. If you're struggling to take action, set a date. This will keep you from ruminating and fuel more urgency.

Powerhouse realtor Charles Velasco also iterates in Episode 18 how the internet has equalized the world. There are no excuses not to act because we have access to information like never before. We can Google or YouTube our way into becoming just about anything. Charles is young, relentless in his pursuit of excellence, and does not hesitate to make decisions that will grow his real estate business. A key takeaway that stuck with me from my interview with Charles was around how having successful systems in place can exponentially help grow your success. Whether it is in your personal or professional life, having systems and processes make a world of difference; an action I encourage you to take that will help you overcome your self-limiting beliefs is to do an inventory of the systems you have in place in your life—e.g., how you get client leads, how you prioritize what tasks you tackle first in your day, how you manage the organization of your household. Building repeatable practices into your life will increase your confidence and whittle away at any self-doubt and limited thinking that may be blocking you.

When your confidence drops below the Self-Belief line (recall the visual on page 46) and your faith is tested, every action that you take is a testament of who you are and what you are made of. The journey back above the Self-Belief line is the path to becoming a better version of yourself. Looking upward to the next mountain can feel daunting and overwhelming, but when you put one foot in front of the other, you will get to the next destination. Key ingredients to action are intuition, accountability, tenacity, and equanimity. The most inspiring example of these ingredients in action is from the 2006 movie, *The Pursuit of Happyness,* starring Will Smith. The movie takes place in San Francisco, California. Chris Gardner invests his entire life savings in portable bone density scanners. He wasn't as successful as he had hoped, and the financial strife he faced took a toll on his marriage. His wife Linda, a hotel maid, eventually leaves for New York to explore the prospect of a potential job.

Everything in Chris's world was crumbling. His career vision was defeated. His marriage was in turmoil. He soon was evicted. Furthermore, Chris was trying to be a motivating force in the life of his five-year old son, Christopher Jr., who remained with him when his wife left. He landed a six-month unpaid internship for Dean Witter Reynolds while homeless. His focus was not on his homelessness; it was on his dream of becoming a stockbroker. Chris had the intuition to listen to his calling. He was accountable for the decisions he made. He had the tenacity to persevere through what was likely the lowest point of his life. Through the storm, he demonstrated equanimity. With this recipe, he won a full-time coveted position at Dean Witter Reynolds. Chris went on to start a multi-million-dollar brokerage firm. From homeless to multi-millionaire—that takes tremendous action.

PROCRASTINATION

Have you fallen victim to procrastination, telling yourself every day or every week that you're going to get something done, yet it remains on your to-do list? I am sure we all have. One of the books that offers great tips is *Procrastinate on Purpose: 5 Permissions to Multiply Your Time* by Rory Vaden. The crux of his book is about what "Multipliers" do—these are people who are able to multiply their time by acting differently than those who struggle with productivity. Here are the highlights of what Rory says that multipliers do differently.

1. Multipliers don't complain about how busy they are. They prioritize their commitments and take ownership of them. Intentionality helps them focus on the tasks that matter.

2. Multipliers don't just focus on tasks; they focus on results. They eliminate timewasters like watching TV and revisiting decisions that have already been made.

3. Multipliers invest versus just spend their money by looking for ways to automate repeatable tasks like setting up autopay for bills or using programs to schedule social media posts.

4. Multipliers delegate; they don't get everything done on their own. They free up their time by outsourcing tasks to other people with the right skill set.

5. Multipliers distinguish what's best to be done now versus later. They do things like batching similar tasks so they can get done at one time more efficiently.

6. Multipliers protect their time, so they have capacity to concentrate on important work that needs to get done. Once concentrating, they avoid distractions like social media.

Do any of these approaches appeal to you? Is there anything in this list that you might try or try more of? It's easy to make excuses and avoid getting important things done, but if you develop habits like a multiplier, it becomes less overwhelming to be productive.

INTUITION

Intuition is something we all have yet underestimate. It is our gut instinct, our sixth sense, and our premonition. It is like when you would take that multiple choice exam, and there are four answer options. You narrow it down to the two best options, and most times, when you follow your intuition, you choose the correct answer. When you overthink, you choose the wrong answer. On the mission to grow beyond your self-limiting beliefs, it is natural to get insights and input from others. Others will have an opinion and advice to give. When left in a quiet room reflecting on all the input you have collected, it is your gut instinct that rules the day. I hear great people who have reached the highest level of their magnificence talk about how the most important answers have come to them in the silence of meditation.

In Episode 58 of my podcast show, I admire how my soul sister Anita Vita describes intuition when sharing her personal story. Anita calls it the quiet whisper. As a burned-out nurse, Anita found meditation and the practice of Qigong as solace and an incredibly powerful healing tool. The quiet whisper showed up for her at various times in her self-exploration voyage, and it is what lit the path to her living in her gifting today—to help others heal, become centered, and be made whole. How beautiful it is to tap into that inner light. Anita's story helps us understand that life is not a straight line. It's more like a zig zag or swirl. It's like climbing a rock wall. There are many ways to get where you want to go. You can change your mind. You can discover something new or have a revelation on your quest that leads you somewhere different than you originally planned. That's what intuition is all about—listening to yourself and following that quiet whisper when it's subtly shifting you toward your destiny.

ACCOUNTABILITY

People seek out coaches or other guides for two main reasons, organization, and accountability. Do not be afraid to connect with someone who can help you stay the course. A professional is a great resource because they do not have an emotional attachment to the circumstances in your life. An outside expert can be a neutral thinker and provide perspective that is unhindered. Experts are a constant in my own life. I turn to therapists, spiritual healers, performance coaches, and business mentors for direction and accountability. I know that without these individuals, I would not have achieved the clarity in my purpose that I have today or the speed at which I have achieved my goals. In fact, to write this book, I had an all-star writing coach, Ashley Mansour, and a whole community of other authors who believed in me to persevere through the authorship process. I went through the stumble and storm of believing I was not worthy of telling my story, and it is the accountability of the communities I put myself in like my author group and mastermind who reminded me constantly of my worth and impact.

The power of someone like a mentor or coach is the preparation they can help you with like anticipating future actions, scheduling activities that empower you to plan ahead like a quarterly retreat or review and choosing automated systems that save you time. The role of an expert could also be for a season where you need direction or a boost or long-term. I have both kind of experts in my life. For example, a writing coach is someone I leverage when I am writing a book, so the need for this expertise is for a specific reason. A performance coach is a role I will leverage more long-term in my life to support my overall continuous improvement.

Speaking of mentorship, one of the podcast guests that I was so impressed by who exemplified taking accountability and action and finding mentorship support was life mastery coach Dennis Berry. I did a two-part interview with him, Episodes 113 and 150. He had a sixteen-year addiction to drugs and alcohol. He nearly died hundreds of times. From car accidents and outrageous benders to waking up disillusioned covered in dried up blood and in the same clothes after several days, he's experienced what many people would call rock bottom multiple times. After a terrible binge, with the encouragement of his girlfriend at the time, Dennis began a remarkable journey from addiction to recovery and sobriety. Dennis has been sober now for nearly two decades, and the most impactful part of his experience is the transformation he's helped countless people to achieve worldwide through his coaching and programs.

Even today, like many, Dennis battles with limiting beliefs of not feeling enough, unworthy, and having imposter syndrome, but he practices mindset work to remind himself that these are merely thoughts, not realities. His accountability to his sobriety has been steadfast. It started with Alcoholics Anonymous (AA), but most importantly, his accountability has been to himself. He changed his inputs which informed the development of better and healthier habits in all the aspects of his life, health, wealth, and relationships. In his darkest hours, he found the courage to ask for help and guidance and is forever grateful that he did. His drug and alcohol addiction are a part of his past, and the life he lives today is magnificent. It is quite the miracle when you consider the countless times he's danced with death.

Whether formal or informal, ask for guidance. Mentorship is an influence that is absolutely worth the investment. The choice of mentorship is undoubtedly a useful one, but the ultimate person you are accountable to is you. It might not be that you turn to another person every time you need accountability. It could be the fire of your purpose that sustains you, the steadfast habits you've committed to, or something else. You'll know when it's time to ask for help, and when that time comes, don't hesitate—just act.

TENACITY

Tenacity is where your purpose and mindset come in. When the conviction of your purpose is strong enough, you will act even in those moments that you don't want to. Your purpose is bigger than you. When there is something bigger that wakes you up in the morning and keeps you inspired, you will find the strength to persevere. A tenacious mindset is one that encourages you with the affirmations that keep you going. Post-its and alarms are two tools that have helped me keep my tenacious spirit alive amidst the negative energy that attempts to pervade my environment. I put positive affirmations where I can see them and set alarms that remind me of who I am. One of my favorite post-it notes says, "You are not responsible for other people's happiness." My wake-up alarm says, "I am an influential mission driven messenger, and I inspire others." My noon alarm says, "The Universe supports me." My 5:00 p.m. alarm says, "I am enough." My partner in crime Aaron even had me set a nighttime alarm to remind me that I am mini, but mighty. I always laugh when that one goes off. In *The Pursuit of Happyness*, it was evident that Chris Gardner's tenacity came from his son. He didn't want his son to wake up on bathroom floors and in homeless shelters for the rest of his life. His conviction was bigger than him, and that drove him every day to act even when it was difficult.

I know *The Pursuit of Happyness* is a bit of an extreme example of someone going from rock bottom to soaring. There's great value in investing into what you are most passionate about. More people may resonate with working on going from mediocrity to excelling and getting to the next level, so I will share with you a personal example which is about not putting all my eggs in one basket. One of the common actions I see people take is investing the bulk of their action and energy in one place. That's not a bad thing, but there could be a ceiling as to how much return they'll get for their investment. As a consultant who works for a professional firm, I could chase every possible promotion. If I was promoted to the highest position, there would still be a cap as to how much of a salary I would make, and additional income could come from sales bonuses.

I've chosen to diversify where I expend my energy. Instead of pouring it into one place and getting to a point where there is a ceiling, I have side hustles where I have the autonomy to control how much effort I put in, can make extra money, and am building a legacy for my future. For the event business that I co-own, renters contribute to paying expenses, there's room for profit, and as the mortgage is paid, equity increases, and over time, my asset (property) appreciates in value. Diversifying gives me new problems to solve, allows me to impact more people, and helps me to hone my skills. Having multiple investments may not be for everyone. It is a path that has been fulfilling to me, and one that you can consider if it suits you.

EQUANIMITY

Finally, *equanimity* has more recently become a word that I admire. The definition of equanimity is "mental calmness, composure, evenness of temper, especially in a difficult situation." In Ed Mylett's book, *The Power of One More*, he has a terrific chapter on equanimity. In Chapter Seventeen, "One More Degree of Equanimity, he says that "we can't control outcomes despite our best efforts," and that when faced with a difficult or stressful situation, "the highest achievers can find equanimity, when others can't." This makes me think of the greats like Buddha, Confucius, the Dalai Lama, Mother Teresa, Dr. Martin Luther King Jr., and Michelle Obama. These are individuals who have had a worldwide impact with their calmness and wisdom. It takes more strength to be level-headed in the face of adversity than it does to choose anger or animosity.

Equanimity is choosing a higher sense of self. We are capable of vibrating at a higher frequency when we have a clear conviction of who we are, maintain a sense of peace and confidence in a noisy and cluttered world, and can go inward in the moments our boundaries get jolted. When I think about habits, equanimity is one I am still learning to practice. As you can see from the references I pay respect to, audiobooks are one of the key inputs that sustain me.

PERFECTIONISM

One dimension to be cautious of is perfectionism. There is no such thing as perfect. Perfect is an enemy to a self-limiting belief because when we hold ourselves to an unreasonable standard, we make it impossible to achieve what we desire. The danger of perfectionism is living in a state of misery, disappointment, negativity, and delay. A great example I can offer is my real estate journey. I started investing in real estate in my early twenties, and since then I've bought and sold five homes. I bought my first property with friends while I was still in college. I didn't know much back then, but I knew enough to know that investing was a smart thing to do because real estate is an asset that appreciates over time. The next investment I made was at twenty-eight in 2011. I put $25,000 down on a $185,000 home in the Bay Area of Northern California. If you know a little bit about the California real estate market, you know it's a market that continues to appreciate. By the time I sold this property eleven years later, it was for more than three times what I purchased it for. The point of this story is that when I started investing, I wasn't a real estate expert.

I knew just enough to make a smart decision, and I kept learning along the way.

If I had spent too long waiting for the perfect time, the perfect market, the perfect interest rate, the perfect strategy, and so on, I would not have been able to acquire the real estate investments I have today where I'm able to make passive income. Investing has become one of the strategies I use to combat the self-limiting belief I had in the past around being limited financially to only what my parents were able to accomplish. Expanding my inputs (what kind of information and education I was feeding my brain) was a huge factor in sustaining the belief I had in myself to be financially successful.

WRITING AND REFLECTION PROMPT: ACT QUESTIONS

1. *What is one goal that you commit to working on daily?*
2. *What system do you need to implement or elevate to achieve the results you desire?*
3. *Who can help hold you accountable for your commitments?*

9

TO ALIGN IS TO BE
UNAPOLOGETICALLY YOU

THE FINAL A (ALIGN) IN the A5 process is one that has taken me the longest to gain a deeper understanding of, and it is the step that I am currently spending the most time learning from. To transcend limited thinking, you must come into alignment with the full essence of who you are, what you believe, and what you stand for. In other words, you want to follow through on your commitments and goals by planning and executing. The cycle of self-limiting beliefs that I shared at the beginning of the book will be ever-present at different junctures of our lives when curve balls get thrown at us and unexpected events occur, but when we come full circle to alignment is when we surrender to the trust we have in ourselves.

At the beginning of each year, I choose a word of intention. MyIntent Project inspires this practice. If you visit the MyIntent Project website (https://myintent.org), you'll learn that a word of intention can be a variety of things like a virtue you want to live more of, a challenge you want to overcome, or something you want to passionately pursue. There's even a word finder quiz if you need help finding a word. If desired, you can order items like a bracelet, necklace, or keychain to remind you of your word and the commitment you have made to it. I chose a necklace. I wear it often.

For 2024, I chose the word *alignment* as my word of intention. It's a reminder to me to be aligned with my values, which are fun, impact, growth, and stability. I sometimes have the habit of saying yes to the wrong things or prioritizing ineffectively. Based on my values, alignment means if I am going to say yes to something, I should be able to say yes to each of these questions:

1. *Am I going to enjoy what I am doing?*
2. *Will what I am doing make the kind of impact that I want it to?*
3. *Will I grow from this experience?*
4. *Will what I am doing make me feel stable?*

The questions you ask yourself will be different based on the things that you personally value. The reason alignment can be challenging is because you continue to evolve.

What you value and believe may change over time, so that brings you back to revisiting your personal life compass: purpose, mindset, habits, inputs, and influences. It starts with accepting who you are and where you are in life. Your compass keeps you aligned to your authentic self.

SELF-ACCEPTANCE

The environment I grew up in did have strong, independent women, which I've always appreciated. There were occasional examples of women who stepped out and spoke their mind even if it went against the majority, but most were agreeable and did not rock the boat. I would characterize myself as diplomatic, conflict-averse, and one who pursues win-win situations, hence why I am a successful coach; I listen well, have empathy, show compassion, and find the good in others. Being a peacekeeper, though, means I am uncomfortable with disagreement and intense debate, particularly with strangers. Every personality assessment I have ever taken highlights how well I do at the soft skills. It really wasn't until my thirties that I embraced all the parts of me, even when others disagree.

I am an extroverted (also described as "extra") multicultural woman and Zumba enthusiast who loves true crime and unicorns, has more tattoos than most corporate leaders you see, does not believe in monogamy, believes in a universal higher power over religion, does not want biological children (for now anyway), enjoys serial entrepreneurship, lives to bring out the best in others, loves the adventure of travel, could eat sushi every day, and has decided to no longer drink alcohol and soda (as mentioned previously) after my fortieth birthday. I meet people who accept me and those who judge me, which is likely no different than you. When judged by people who are closest to you, it is disappointing. I do think non-acceptance can make us question ourselves. It certainly has made me question myself.

What I have come to embrace is something I heard Karamo Brown from *Queer Eye* talk about on a podcast interview with actress Sophia Bush, which is that not everyone needs to be in "the front row seat of our lives." There are friends and loved ones who may need to move to the balcony seats. I've heard a few other sayings that I love. One of my accountability partners, happiness coach Erika, says, "You are not everyone's cup of tea." People like different teas and that's okay. My favorite is when I am in the nail salon (which is basically a way more fun means of therapy and sometimes even group therapy) and differing opinions emerge about the way to do life. Eric, one of my nail techs, will top off an especially provocative conversation with, "Do you, Boo Boo!" Damn right, Eric, I will do me; I needed to hear that, thank you.

Remember when I referenced the Netflix series *Sex/ Life*, where I was pleased that the main character Billie in the show thoroughly assessed her life to make the bold decision to end her nine-year marriage against popular opinion (including the opinion of her own mother)? Well, the assess stage comes back full circle with align stage of the A5 (Assess, Analyze, Adjust, Act, Align) process. In season one, the series ends with Billie at a crossroads assessing the direction she wanted to go.

In season two, Billie aligned her behaviors and actions with the new life she wanted to live for herself. She moved into her own place, coordinated a schedule for when she would spend time with her kids, pursued her PhD, enjoyed dating, bonded with her best friend, and found her way back to her first love (spoiler alert if you haven't watched it!). Her epiphany and awakening were to live a life that meant being a mom, excelling in her career, *and* having a deep, passionate partnership. Her self-acceptance was the catalyst to how she got aligned with her goals and cultivated a life of her own volition despite what anybody else thought about her. That's what I want for all of you—to wake up every morning saying to yourself, "This is the life that I designed, and I am living it EXACTLY the way I want to, unapologetically."

SAVERS

The people that can have front row tickets to your life are SAVERs. A SAVER is a person who supports you, is aligned with you, value-adds to your life, elevates you, and rises with you. A person who supports you will believe in your dreams, encourage you to pursue them, challenge your limiting beliefs, and show up in the tough times, not just the bright moments. Being aligned pertains to having shared goals and aspirations and respect for one another's beliefs. Value-add means bringing wisdom, resources, meaningful experiences, and includes the act of giving not only receiving. A person who brings you elevation uplifts you to new levels in life. One who rises is looking to grow and develop just like you are. SAVERs influence you positively. Evaluate the people who are SAVERs in your life and be honest with yourself if you need to expand this group.

My sister Diane is a prime example of a SAVER in my life. She always looks for the bright spots in situations. In the lowest of low moments in my life, she has not judged me and has always encouraged me. I also appreciate her brutal honesty. She doesn't sugarcoat anything. We can talk about the good, bad, and the ugly, but we always arrive at what actions it will take to make circumstances better. She doesn't stay stuck in the muck. The most meaningful part of our relationship is that we share our goals and aspirations with one another. We both motivate each other to reach our best potential. We've committed to each other that through the ups and downs of life, we can lean on each other.

DRAINERS

The people that you want to steer clear of are DRAINERs. A DRAINER is someone who **d**iscriminates you, has a **r**esentful attitude, provokes **a**nxiety, is **i**nconsiderate, has a negative outlook, exhausts you, and is resistant to change. Discrimination is related to judgment. A person who judges other people is narrow-minded and lives in a world where things are only "right" when they're done on terms they believe in. Any differing opinion is cause for discrimination. A resentful person sees the glass as half empty not half full. This is a person who focuses on everything that they don't have instead of being grateful for everything they do have.

A DRAINER makes you feel anxiety when you engage in conversation with them because you anticipate their negative energy. This is a person who consistently considers their feelings above yours (inconsiderate). This is the kind of person whose negativity exhausts you and who is not willing to change but expects the people around them to adapt to their standards and beliefs.

Do you have a DRAINER in your life? Just as important as it is to bring SAVERs into your life, it's equally important to examine any DRAINERs in your life so you can distance yourself or eliminate them. If you want to work through any limiting beliefs, you must align yourself with people who fuel your energy, not deplete it. I am a firm believer that you either have anchors or sails in your life. A DRAINER is an anchor who holds you back from becoming the best version of yourself. A SAVER is someone who helps you sail towards your goals and aspirations. What would your life look like if you were surrounded by a group full of SAVERs? Imagine the kind of momentum you would have.

HEALING

Have you ever heard the phrases "hurt people hurt people" and "healed people heal people?" I do believe there is truth to these statements. It feels like I have spent a lifetime healing from past wounds. I found myself in therapy on multiple occasions to heal from relationships in strife and self-sabotage. I have spent years reading books and joining communities of people who can empower me. I have connected with myself spiritually through practices such as yoga and meditation. It took me until thirty-two years old to wholeheartedly love myself, accept my mistakes, and give myself grace. Today, I continue to be a part of groups that keep me accountable to living in my purpose. I don't claim omnipotence. I remain a student of life, and that keeps me open to new possibilities.

As you embark on the healing experience, remember that it's up to you how you invite others to be a part of your healing process. Think of yourself as a peaceful home with a fence around it built for safety and protection. Any hurtful, harmful, or negative energy that comes to your fence can be denied entry. That's a healthy boundary you can set. When there are disruptive people attempting to enter your orbit of healing, consider this question: *Would you trade places with that person?* If you would not trade places with a person, that is usually a good indication of where you should be placing them in your life. You may need to exercise crucial conversation skills to support how you communicate and set boundaries. In the book *Crucial Conversations* by Joseph Grenny, Kerry Patterson, et al., there are three ways you can approach a difficult conversation with someone characterized by the acronym CPR:

1. C = content—first you reference a single event or situation
2. P = pattern—then you can evolve to discussing a pattern of recurring behavior
3. R = relationship—finally, you engage on how behavior impacts your relationship

By focusing on facts using one or several of these communication approaches, you can intentionally protect your peace that allows you to heal in a healthy way.

Healing is a process that takes time, and you don't need to rush through it. The danger of moving too swiftly through the healing process or underestimating the time it takes to go through the healing process is carrying remnants of pain, disbelief, doubt, shame, guilt, and rumination with you wherever you go. This feels like carrying a backpack full of rocks, and it takes a toll on you. It's tiring. You may get triggered and agitated easily. This will impact how you show up in relationships, react in situations that test you, and creates a barrier blocking you from overcoming any self-limiting beliefs. Take the time to go through the five stages of grief, determine what it takes for you to forgive yourself and others, find the spaces that make you feel safe, journal your thoughts, feelings, and growth, and leverage the formal and informal support systems you need to maintain a state of healthy wholeness.

When I needed professional emotional support and guidance, I turned to the Employee Assistance Program (EAP) at my firm. I was fortunate to have a set number of therapy sessions covered as a benefit each calendar year. I didn't realize until I went through therapy a few times how helpful it was. Sometimes self-limiting beliefs are so deep-seated that it takes an outsider looking in to help you heal and overcome. If you do have an employer, EAP may be a part of your benefits. It's worth investigating!

In therapy is where I was able to explore the difficulties and roadblocks I had in relationships. Therapists were able to hear me talk about patterns of relationships I attracted and behaviors I tended to exhibit in different scenarios or emotional states. I had a habit of attracting relationships with people I thought I could fix, save, or change. I also tended to fall in love with people's potential instead of their reality, meaning I could see who they could become and focused on a future version of a person instead of the one standing right in front of me. I was a serial optimist. I had to get real with myself about how to change my habits and behaviors if I wanted to experience relationships differently. If I didn't want to go through bouts of narcissism, co-dependence, unhealthy emotional attachment, mental manipulation, and gaslighting, I had to make change and setting boundaries a priority. There is no shame in seeking mental health support.

Professionals can help you see your life through a different lens. Sometimes the lens you are looking through is limited and doesn't show you the full picture, which means you could be missing important angles that have repeatedly put you in the same cycle of behaviors that no longer serve you for where you are in life. My first round of therapy, as previously highlighted, helped me understand who I was attracting and how I was behaving in romantic relationships. In a different season of my life, therapy helped me realize what caused the tension and friction in the relationship I had with my mother. We are polar opposite people. I kept agonizing over why my mother wasn't more like me instead of accepting her for who she was. When I stopped resisting our differences and accepted that we are unique individuals who see the world differently, I was able to focus on how to set the right boundaries that would help us have a healthy relationship.

BOUNDARIES

Speaking of boundaries, a few years ago, I discovered the book *Boundaries: When to Say Yes, How to Say No to Take Control of Your Life* by Henry Cloud and John Townsend.

It was lifechanging. I did not know what a boundary truly was until I read this book. Your battle with self-limiting beliefs will be harder if you don't learn how to exercise boundaries. Physical, mental, and emotional boundaries allow us to preserve our energy, protect our peace, and keep ourselves from situations that may involve manipulation, narcissism, and gas-lighting. Others can use guilt, ego, self-ishness, and pressure to control our psychology, and the more you stand convicted in your purpose and core beliefs, the better you will be able to walk away and, in some cases, even cut off people in your life who are no longer serving you. Remember that you only live one life, so don't let others rob you of your energy, time, or joy. I spoke earlier about how we can project our thoughts and beliefs onto others. People can do the same to you. Don't let other people's projections stop you from living the life that is meant for you. You get what you tolerate, so don't tolerate less than what you know that you deserve.

Now, in the decade of my forties, I have been much more diligent about boundaries. I can count at least a handful of relationships that are no longer present in my life because they were not serving me. Think about a person in your life today who drains you—they take energy rather than fuel you, have a negative outlook on life, and question your every move because they have a fixed instead of a growth mindset. When you finish a visit with this person or hang up the phone with them, how do you feel?

If the answer is that you feel exhausted, you may need to exercise better boundaries to keep him or her at a distance.

I hate to be the one to break it to you, but boundaries apply to your family too. Trust me, I know this all too well. Here are some statements to consider as you are evaluating who you may need to exercise stricter boundaries on in your life. Rate each statement on a 1–5 scale where 1 means never, 3 means sometimes, and 5 means always. Do this separately for each person you want to assess.

Question	Rating
I feel heard, seen, and acknowledged in this relationship.	
I feel reciprocity in this relationship (a balance of give and take).	
I feel encouraged and uplifted by our conversations.	
I feel like this person helps me to think bigger and more creatively.	
I trust that that this person always has my best interest in mind.	
I see this person consistently conquering their self-limiting beliefs.	
I admire this individual, and they motivate me to grow and be better.	

If scores are mostly 3 or less, then you've got actions to take to step up your boundaries. For all the time and energy you spend on relationships that aren't serving you and depleting you of your energy, you're minimizing the capacity for you to make room for the relationships that will positively impact your life. Relationships are an investment. You wouldn't place your bets on stocks or other investments that would yield you a negative return, so why wouldn't you treat your relationships similarly? Don't let a relationship cause you emotional bankruptcy. Choose your investments wisely.

IMPACT

When you are in service of others, the work you do will pay dividends in ways you don't anticipate. When I stopped making life just about me is when I opened myself up to deeper fulfillment and happiness. Doing volunteer work and coaching others are reminders that the world is much bigger than me and my adversities. Examples such as building houses domestically and abroad for Habitat for Humanity International (Habitat), serving on the Disaster Action Team for the Red Cross in Northern California, and volunteering at homeless and domestic violence centers took me outside of my own circumstances to serve others in need.

My first Habitat trip was to Guatemala. I spent ten days immersed in the Guatemalan culture—its environment, its language, its food, its people, its history, and its traditions. Day after day, another piece of my heart was taken as I learned about and bonded with one of the families we were building a home for. If this is the first time you've heard about Habitat, it's an international organization founded in 1976 that has the mission of bringing people together to build homes, communities, and hope. Homes are built by volunteers and the recipients of the home (usually five hundred hours of "sweat equity"). Financial support comes from national governments, philanthropic foundations, corporations, and mass media companies. There's an extensive application process for any family who applies for a Habitat home.

The family I worked with had gratitude beyond what I had ever experienced. It was the first time they would ever live independently. They were insistent about the way my fellow builders and I changed their lives. What I hope they realized was how much they changed mine. The Habitat volunteer experience expanded my view of the world and what one individual could do to make a difference in the world. You will not feel limited if you open your heart to serving others. Impact is the ultimate fulfillment. If you ever find yourself stuck in a self-limiting mindset, consider the impact you could be making far beyond yourself and see what kind of encouragement that brings you to breakthrough.

One of the best examples I have seen of someone living in their alignment is Amanda Foo-Ryland, who is an international speaker and author. I interviewed her on my podcast show where she dialed in from beautiful Portugal. She has this incredible TED Talk on Label-less Living that you must look up on YouTube. In Episode 118, she talked about the damage that labels can do to us. She shared her personal experience with cancer, sexuality, and reprogramming her neurology through the power of language and thoughts. This helped her to manifest a more fulfilling and abundant life. She chose not to accept the labels other people placed on her. She referred to herself as simply Amanda. I love that. Each of us is a unique being. Why be like everyone else when you can be one of a kind?

WRITING AND REFLECTION PROMPT: ALIGN QUESTIONS

1. *What healing work do you need to do?*
2. *What boundaries do you need to set or expand and with whom?*
3. *Who are the SAVERs and DRAINERs in your life?*

10

THE CULMINATION

THE JOURNEY OF BORN UNBREAKABLE has taught me that we are all capable of surviving the bumps, bruises, and scrapes in life. The guests I have interviewed are living proof that not only can you get to the other side of self-doubt, uncertainty, fear, and limitations, but you can achieve in life things that are beyond your wildest imagination in health, wealth, and relationships. Self-limiting beliefs will be triggered in our lives, but by using the tool of our personal compass to keep us grounded in who we are and the A5 process, we can build our resilience faster and bounce back from any setback.

Wherever you are on your journey, I see you. You are not alone. Honor where you are. You are right where you need to be. You are ready for what's next. Be exactly who you are. Appreciate what you have learned. Enjoy the process of growing. Be intentional about choosing your tribe. The culmination of your life experiences has gotten you this far. Remember, you did not come this far only to come this far. With the A5 framework, you can thrive! Here's a few more guiding principles to ensure you stay the course.

START WITH WHY

There's a reason that purpose is at the center of the personal compass. It serves as your true north star. A decade ago, author and optimist Simon Sinek wrote the book *Start with Why: How Great Leaders Inspire Everyone to Take Action*. He highlights how the greatest leaders like Martin Luther King Jr., Steve Jobs, and the Wright Brothers, while very different, all started with *Why*. He introduces the powerful idea of The Golden Circle. It is comprised of three circles—Why (center), How (middle circle), and What (outer circle). *How* is about the specific actions taken to realize your why. *What* is about your result. *Why* (most important of all) is about your purpose, motivation, and what you believe. Great leaders communicate from the inside out, from their heart, and therefore stories are the catalyst that moves people into action. People are compelled by what tugs at their heart strings or matters most to them. For example, look at the brand Resera (https://www.resera.com). Resera is a jewelry company that exists to employ and empower women overcoming homelessness and domestic violence situations.

Their jewelry is beautiful, but the reason I bought it when I saw it displayed at a self-development and networking event I attended in Nashville, Tennessee, is because of the story behind it. We all have a story and a *Why* within us. It's what attracts people to you and what you stand for. When you're feeling lost, misaligned, or undetermined, connecting back to your purpose will help you stay on track.

At the event in Nashville, I had the pleasure of meeting three-time Olympic Gold Medalist of the U.S.A. Softball Team Leah Amico. She was one of the event speakers. I interviewed her in Episode 134 of my podcast show. Purpose was one of the driving forces behind her Olympic mindset in addition to three other Ps that she shared—passion, persistence, and preparation. That's a powerful combination of an unstoppable mindset. It's that mindset that helped Leah to perform under the pressure of the Olympic stage.

One of the things Leah said that stuck with me was: "Always play to win; never play not to lose." She was referring to playing offensively versus defensively. When it comes to self-limiting beliefs, this is a great way to think. Keep it simple. Reframe your limited thought from "I can't" to "How can I?" When you assume you can't do something, you've already predicted a negative outcome. When you tell yourself that you *can* do something, even if the outcome is less than ideal, you can be proud that you were brave enough to try. This adjustment in thinking is when you unleash manifestation.

MANIFESTING

Do you believe in manifestation? Manifesting is about willing and conjuring into existence the things that you want. One of the most popular works around manifestation is the book and documentary *The Secret* by Rhonda Byrne. The book focuses on the law of attraction and how you can attract what you want in every aspect of your life—money, health, relationships, and happiness—through the power of your mindset. Through centuries of teachings from ancient to modern day, evidence shows that believing is achieving. Byrne promotes a three-step process: ask, believe, receive.

Manifestation includes practicing gratitude and visualization. In its most simple form, manifesting is getting back from the universe what you put out. If you emanate positivity, you get positivity in return. If you emanate negativity, you get negativity in return. How might I apply manifestation to my self-limiting beliefs? Let's take "I am unworthy of love because I have been divorced." I would flip that statement on its head to put into the universe a new narrative with statements such as:

> *I emanate love; therefore, I am surrounded by an abundance of love.*
>
> *I am love and am open to receiving love.*

I am blessed for the opportunity to experience multiple love stories.

I enjoy the process of loving others wholeheartedly.

I am grateful for the love that continues pouring into my life.

These statements are positive. I have adopted a new narrative, and that's why today I've been blessed with experiences of love beyond what I could have ever imagined for myself. Manifesting is one way to shift your vibration. If you are skeptical, give manifestation a try. Take the self-limiting belief you're working through and write down the new narrative you'd like to make a reality. If you put it on something like a post-it, then you can place the statement where you can see it daily. I personally am a fan of the daily alarm. You can set the time and the tone. Whatever you decide, be intentional and choose what works best for you. Remember that if ever you don't like your story, you have the power to re-write it.

In Episode 54 of my podcast show, I interviewed Manifestation Coach Judith Joy. Following her divorce, she changed her last name to Joy, and she has spent over two decades immersed in energy healing and studying how the heart and mind work together. From her studies, she invented a simple four-step manifestation process: 1) be high vibe by aiming for the highest possible vibration for the greatest ease, 2) imagine your dream by clarifying your desire, what it looks like, and what it will feel like when completed, 3) ask and let it go by knowing what you truly desire, asking for it, and surrendering it to the universe, and 4) prepare to receive by clearing away anything that gets in the way and doesn't work. I love the simplicity of these four steps. You can add this to your toolbox if you're struggling with a self-limiting belief. Changing your language and then speaking what you want into the universe can result in powerful results for you.

One of the books I recommend that will help you through manifestation exploration is *The Alchemist* by author Paulo Coelho. The plot is about a shepherd boy named Santiago who is on a voyage to find the meaning of a recurring dream that he's having. He is given a prophecy that he will discover treasure at the Egyptian pyramids. He meets many people on his quest. One of his encounters is with a wise alchemist who teaches him to realize his true self. The main message of the book is that when you really want something, the universe conspires to make your wish a reality. The most powerful message in the book is that your "Personal Legend" is lived by being open to finding your destiny in unexpected places and living in the present moment. It is in the present that you appreciate and absorb everything around you. Soak in every zig and every zag of life and know the universe is conspiring in your favor.

SURRENDER

In Episode 142 of my podcast show, I interview success coach Shane Flanagan. He's the author of the book *Shades of Broken*, and he helps people to achieve clarity, balance, and success. One day on the law enforcement job that he loved, he experienced a traumatizing incident. Soon after, he was diagnosed with post-traumatic stress disorder (PTSD), which does not just occur from situations of combat like often depicted in movies and TV shows. PTSD can result from shocking, scary, or dangerous life events, which is what Shane experienced. His traumatizing experience in the police force led him on a spiritual journey where he surrendered to learning from many healers (doctors, therapists, a life coach, and other spiritual teachers). Surrendering to learning, growth, and expansion is what helped Shane work through limiting beliefs that came up for him, especially around having PTSD.

What does surrender look like for you in your journey to overcoming your self-limiting beliefs? For Shane, it was a spiritual voyage. Surrendering is about releasing the tension and friction in your life and opening yourself up to exploring answers to questions that you have—especially questions that get to the root cause of where your self-limiting beliefs stem from. When you understand the root cause, the A5 (Assess, Analyze, Adjust, Act, Align) process of unpacking it can begin—assess where you are and where you want to be, analyze the data points that will help take you in the direction you want to go, adjust incrementally to the behaviors that will make you successful, act with intention, and align your actions to your why/purpose.

Failure can be a source of surrender, because when we experience failure, it's an opportunity to surrender to new approaches and possibilities. *New York Times* bestselling author John C. Maxwell wrote the book, *Failing Forward: Turning Mistakes into Stepping Stones for Success.* The essence of the book is around deconditioning ourselves from the fear of failure. Failure is simply learning.

When I bought my Las Vegas investment property in 2022, the intent was to use the property for Airbnb and events to make passive income. Within the first ninety days, I received a notice that I would be fined if I continued to run my short-term rental without the proper license due to a complaint from a lovely neighbor we'll call Karen. At the time, I already had a business license but didn't complete the process for the additional requirement of a short-term rental license. I was still not making a profit at the time, and the city was taking away a source of income that was helping me to pay my mortgage. For a little additional insight, the interest rate on an investment property mortgage is higher than a primary home mortgage because lenders see investments as a higher risk profile.

So, was my investment a failure? No, it was an opportunity to pivot cash-flowing strategies. Could this pursuit conjure up the limiting belief that I was not meant to be an entrepreneur in the short-term rental space? Absolutely, but I did not let that happen. I failed forward. Instead of focusing on what didn't work, I focused on what could work better. The stipulation in the short-term rental licensing for the city of Las Vegas was that if you obtained the license, it would be strictly for stays, and no events would be permitted.

Learning about the strict stays-only rule meant that the niche I'd now go after was events, which would be more lucrative anyway. Within a month of pivoting, my partner Aaron and I were getting bookings for corporate events, birthday parties, special events, and wedding receptions with limited marketing…but wait, there's more. Remember Karen, the friendly (and by friendly, I facetiously mean malicious) neighbor? Well, that seemingly bored and not well-intended human decided to continue to complain to any entity that would listen about our occasional events (we are talking about two to four per month). The short version of the story is that we learned from the city we would have to get re-zoned from residential to commercial, which meant a substantial amount of work and money. This was a second major roadblock to cash flow. I am sure you're eagerly wondering what we decided to do next. Where there is a will, there is a way! Aaron and I pivoted to focus on our production business that we already had a business license for too. Customers could rent our sound, lighting, and event equipment, which was finally something that would not aggravate our welcoming (*insert sarcastic tone*) neighbor. We're continuing to find ways to grow our client base.

We had to pivot more than once to figure out how to fund our investment. If you look for solutions and not excuses, you're giving yourself the chance to innovate and write a new destiny that transcends any limitations that once may have gotten in your way.

NEVER GIVE UP

Earlier, I explained the notion of tenacity and what it takes to keep waking up each day in fulfillment of your purpose and vision for life. It's one thing to be motivated when everything is going well, at the beginning of the overcoming journey, or when you're on the upward trajectory of a comeback. What about when things aren't going well? What about when you hit roadblocks, encounter naysayers, experience significant pivots in your plan, have losses, receive complaints, lose money, lose hope, feel like you're hitting rock bottom, or all the above? Time after time, you'll come face to face with a self-limiting belief. It's inevitable. It's when you get back up after being knocked down that the belief in yourself becomes unwavering. The *Rocky* and *Creed* movies are the perfect example of never giving up.

In *Creed II*, the protagonist, American boxer Adonis Creed, is faced with the opportunity to fight against Soviet fighter Viktor Drago, son of Ivan Drago. Ivan killed Adonis's father, Apollo Creed, during a bout a few decades back. Adonis's trainer, mentor, and friend Rocky Balboa defeated Ivan following Apollo's death. Adonis faced internal turmoil feeling like he too could fulfill a revenge by taking on this fight. His battle within rages on throughout the film, and ultimately, he decides to take on the fight. Adonis's decision was driven by purpose and legacy strengthened by his latest role of new father. He was carrying on a legacy of the Creed name but beginning a new legacy of his own for his family. There were many times after making the decision to fight that he wanted to give up, but he never let his fire die out. He not only fought his hardest fight with all his might, but he won.

Another story that moved me is from Brandon T. Adams, two-time Emmy Award–winning producer and entrepreneur. Between the interview he did on my podcast show and learning more about his and his wife's story, I was blown away by their sheer determination. Before he met his wife, Samantha Rossin, she struggled with drug addiction and was in an abusive relationship. It took a colossal amount of courage and faith for her to leave a situation that, although painful, was what she knew and grew accustomed to for so long. Brandon was on a quest for self-discovery too when he and Sam crossed paths. Together, they went through a rollercoaster ride and at one point nearly lost it all: their house, car, businesses—and their faith. They sold everything and started from ground zero, literally from scratch. With faith, determination, and the experiences they acquired, brick by brick they started over.

Brandon and Sam have shot for the stars and catapulted into phenomenal success. They produced *Success in Your City*, which was released on Amazon Prime in 2019 and bspoketv and DirectTV in the fall of 2022. They authored the book *The Road to Success: How to Achieve Success in Business, Life, and Love*. Amongst the many ventures they are involved in, one of the most impactful events they host is called Rise & Record, where they bring together powerhouses who are blazing trails in the video and marketing arena. If Brandon and Sam decided to throw in the towel, they would have missed out not only on the epic success they've achieved, but the major impact they have had on people around the world. At the point you feel like you're about to break or even feel broken already is usually when you are just two millimeters or 1 percent away from a greatness that will forever change your world. So, never give up. Don't let the world miss out on your magic.

LEAVING A LEGACY

What's the most profound part of why making a commitment to overcoming your self-limiting beliefs is paramount? It's the legacy you are creating and will one day leave behind. That's the crux of the culmination. What is a legacy? The formal definition is "the long-lasting impact of particular events, actions, etc. that took place in the past, or of a person's past." Another way I like to think about it is: When you are no longer here, what would someone be saying at your eulogy? It may sound odd, but I think about this more often than might be expected. Death has happened around me at a surprisingly high rate. It feels like every month I hear about a death of a distant relative, an acquaintance from the past, a community member, or someone famous.

I was hit hard by the death of Stephen Laurel "tWitch" Boss. tWitch is most known for being Ellen DeGeneres's DJ on her daytime TV show *Ellen* and being a contestant on the hit TV show *So You Think You Can Dance (SYTYCD)*. tWitch was an amazing freestyle hip hop dancer, choreographer, actor, TV producer, and TV personality. He was beloved by everyone he touched. He was the epitome of light because he lit up every room he walked into. He met his wife, Allison Holker (also a dancer), on the show *SYTYCD*. He left behind three beautiful kids, Weslie, Zaia, and Maddox. He lost his life by suicide. He was reported missing by his wife on December 13, 2022, because he had left their home without taking his car and soon thereafter was found shot at the Oak Tree Inn in Encino, Los Angeles. He was discovered because he missed his check-out time.

tWitch was one of the last people I could imagine taking his own life. Outwardly, it appeared that he had a life anyone would want—a beautiful family, an astounding career, unbelievable talent, and global impact. What we didn't know or see was what he was experiencing on the inside. We can only speculate why tWitch decided to end his life. I've tried hard not to focus on why he left and rather on what he left behind, and that was undoubtedly an unforgettable legacy. He'll be forever remembered and revered for the laughter, light, and love he brought to every human he touched. I only wish whatever limitation was blocking him on the inside is one he would have gotten more support with. I am grateful to have been inspired by his legacy.

In March 2023, a home-town local legend where I grew up in Fremont, California named Jeffrey "JV" Vandergrift went missing and was discovered dead in the San Francisco Bay near Pier 39, a bay area landmark. JV was a long-time disc jockey for the radio station, WiLD 94.9. JV revealed in the last years of his life what it was like to suffer with Lyme disease. He's another example of someone who left behind a legacy of helping and encouraging people through the ups and downs of life through laughter, honest conversations, and music. He was a person known for bringing people together and radiating realness to the world around him. I'm sad that he left the world the way he did but happy he'll be remembered for the person that he was.

One of my favorite legacies still being built by someone who is living as this book is being written. That is the legacy of former president of the United States, Barack Obama. This mention is not meant as a political plug or intended to cause any kind of divisiveness. It is simply my observation of a man who I admire for what he stands for and how he unified a country that has gone in and out of divide throughout its 246-year history. In his *New York Times* bestseller, *A Promised Land*, Barack Obama shares his presidential memoirs of being the first Black president of the United States of America. He was on an odyssey searching for his identity to lead the free world, and through over eight years of leadership, he has left a sensational legacy of grass roots activism, faith in love and harmony, and belief that after every storm, there is hope for change.

Mr. Obama is known for his poise, swag, decorum, intellect, and being nothing short of an international trailblazer. If I met Barack Obama (and of course his inspiring wife, Michelle Obama), my life would be complete (no exaggeration). These are two individuals who have weathered global storms and have been examples of taking the high road with tact, finesse, and equipoise.

No matter how and when I depart from this place we call Earth, when I think about my legacy, I want to be remembered as someone who never gave up, who was true to who she was, who was passionate in her pursuits, who turned lemons into lemonade, who uplifted others, who brought betterment into people's lives, who emulated tenacity and grit, who found fun in everything she did, and who crushed her self-limiting beliefs. I am working on this legacy. Every time things get tough, it's legacy that

I come back to so I can push forward. I am also learning to embrace the battle wounds of life and navigating how these will impact the legacy I leave behind. Our resilience strengthens our resolve and capability of overcoming self-limiting beliefs.

As I write this book, I am in Brené Brown's proverbial arena. I am being tested personally and professionally. The complex needs of my clients are changing and growing, the start-up of our production business, AVA Media & Productions, is in the throes of all that a start-up brings, my mind and body are exhausted, and my mountain of goals is overwhelming. I am stepping through the A5 (Assess, Analyze, Adjust, Act, Align) process now. I have been down rocky roads before, so I am not in a completely unfamiliar territory. I am learning to be okay with not having all the answers. I'm on the alchemist voyage just like Santiago. I'm present, open, and living in my Personal Legend. I relish in the imperfection and embrace that every step in my story, the high points, and the low points, are what got me where I am today. I am grateful for that because it means I am that much closer to stepping into my next reinvention.

I experienced a second divorce in the spring of 2023. I hesitated to share this, but I would be remiss if I didn't. The experience is a part of my legacy. The choice to transition our relationship was about growing into the people we needed to become, which we were unable to do in a marriage. The process has taught me about healthy transition, the power of friendship, the beauty of grace, and the importance maturity. My ex and I have grown in ways neither of us likely thought were possible, and we've shared the most beautiful and profound and heartfelt conversations with each other about love, life, loss, and learning. He's a person I respect dearly and am forever grateful for. He's taught me that love is possible after heartbreak, that pursuing excellence is a life-long journey, that mistakes will be ever-present, and that what matters in life are the bonds that we build. Our love story is a part of my legacy and has helped me embrace the passionate, spontaneous, free-spirited person that I am.

An additional reflection I have about legacy are two spectacular women who have shown me what it means to leave a lasting and impactful legacy are the beautiful and passionate hosts of the wildly popular podcasts, *Root of Evil* and *Facing Evil*, Rasha Pecoraro and Yvette Gentile. It was an honor that I interviewed them both on my podcast show in Episode 111. On January 15, 1947, the gruesomely murdered body of Elizabeth Short (also known as the Black Dahlia) was found in Los Angeles. Rasha and Yvette's great grandfather, George Hodel, was a suspect in the murder, and he was accused of other horrendous acts including incest with his daughter, Tamar Hodel. Rasha and Yvette tell the story of their dark family past and the journey to sharing their mom Fauna Hodel's story of finding light through the darkness in the incredible TV series, *I Am the*

Night starring Chris Pine, India Eisley, and Jefferson Mays. They open up about their personal growth and healing. We have our Hawaiian upbringing in common. They exude the aloha spirit. They did not let their dreadful family past paint the picture of their future. They are changing history by shaping a new and positive legacy of the Hodel name, one that represents strength, love, hope, and healing. You too, have the power to leave a legacy of your choosing.

What do you want your legacy to be? How do you want to be remembered? What would you want someone to say at your eulogy? As you reflect on the self-limiting beliefs that you're working through right now, consider how your purpose and your legacy play a role. When the world gets noisy, find the quiet calm within. It's within where you realize that you are not without. The strength, the fortitude, the fire, the excellence, and most of all your story is found in that sacred ground. A5 (Assess, Analyze, Adjust, Act, Align) is simply the tool that will lead you on the path back to clarity during times when you stray. When in doubt, Assess, Analyze, Adjust, Act, and Align. The time to live an unlimited life is NOW!

WEBSITE REFERENCES

1. WO3 (https://www.wo3connect.com)—a grass-roots movement dedicated to supporting women-owned businesses in three ways: partner, promote, and support.
2. Born Unbreakable (https://bornunbreakable.com)—a brand dedicated to helping people overcome their self-limiting beliefs and live an unapologetic life.
3. 988 Suicide & Crisis Lifeline (https://988lifeline.org)—provides 24/7, free, and confidential support for people in distress, prevention and crisis resources for you or your loved ones, and best practices for professionals in the United States.
4. The DiSC® Assessment (https://www.discprofile.com)—examines how an individual ranks in four primary personality types: dominance, influence, steadiness, and conscientiousness.
5. Strengths Finder (https://www.gallup.com/cliftonstrengths)—measures thirty-four research-

validated talents; themes then guide the development of those talents into strengths to succeed at work and in life.

6. Attachment Style Quiz (https://www.attachment-project.com/attachment-style-quiz)—explores how childhood conditioning manifests into your adult relationships in these four styles: anxious, avoidant, disorganized, or secure.

7. Love Languages Test (https://5lovelanguages.com/quizzes/love-language)—examines how an individual prefers to receive love: through words of affirmation, physical touch, quality time, gifts, or acts of service.

8. 16Personalities Test (https://www.16personalities.com)—determines the dominant personality type amongst sixteen types highlighting what drives, inspires, and worries each.

9. Management by Strengths (https://strengths.com)—assesses temperament, communication style, what motivates individuals, and how each temperament reacts in work and social settings.

10. Hogan Assessment (https://www.hoganassessments.com)—measures everyday strengths, how strengths manifest in times of stress, and values to predict future workplace performance.

11. MyIntent Project (https://myintent.org/)—a catalyst for meaningful conversations and positive interactions.

12. Resera (https://www.resera.com)—a jewelry company that exists to employ and empower women overcoming homelessness and domestic violence situations.

ACKNOWLEDGMENTS

To my family, Darlene, Diane, Rob, Jasmine, and Jacqui, for being on the rollercoaster ride of life with me, especially through every transition. You've been patient, loving, understanding, and encouraging. I am eternally grateful.

To my partner in crime, Aaron, for your honest critiques, innovative ideas, daily humor, unyielding partnership, and fervent commitment to betterment. You always willingly listen. You understand me like no one else does. I can't thank you enough.

To my dear friends and extended family, Katie, Lindsay, Donna, Monique, Maxine, Tammi, Sebastian, Noah, Jason, Angelica, Rick, Norma, Vanessa, and my hula ohana, for your support. You accept me without judgment and lend an ear whenever I need it.

To my mentors and coaches, April, Ashley, Tonia, Ronnie, Jackie, and Penn, for your guidance and wisdom along the way. I'm more resilient, confident, and entrepreneurial because of you. I appreciate you making me better personally and professionally.

To my mastermind family, Bethany, Erica, Christopher, Nick, Nichole, Lauren, Kim, Ben, and Kristen, for your inspiration and passion. You are mission driven messengers, and I can't help but be motivated by you.

To my clients and colleagues for showing me that there is no problem too complex to solve. It is because of each of you that my mission, vision, and values are clear, and I always come back to connecting with purpose.

To my kickboxing community for reminding me every day that bad-assery is a real thing, and it's within each of us. You have reinvigorated the value of community in my life. I am more balanced because of you.

ABOUT THE AUTHOR

Photo by Kate Gardner

DESIREE MAYA IS A CERTIFIED transformational coach, business consultant, change expert, and podcaster. She is the founder of Born Unbreakable and co-host of the *Born Unbreakable Podcast Show*. She has a bachelor's degree in political science and minor in healthcare and social issues from the University of California, San Diego. She is credentialed by the International Coach Federation. Her mission is to help people overcome their self-limiting beliefs and embrace their authenticity. She is passionate about inspirational leadership, self-development, and diversity, equity, and inclusion. Her personal interests are podcasting, real estate investing, true crime, kickboxing, and Zumba. Dez was born and raised in Northern California (the Bay Area) and currently resides in Las Vegas, Nevada. For more information about Dez and how to work with her, please visit https://bornunbreakable.com/.